Relationship Building & Sexual Awareness

for Kids with Autism

S·T·A·R·S 2

Susan Heighway, MS, PNP-BC, APNP &
Susan Kidd Webster, MSSW, ISW

Relationship Building & Sexual Awareness for Kids with Autism:
S·T·A·R·S 2

All marketing and publishing rights guaranteed to and reserved by:

FUTURE HORIZONS INC.

721 W Abram St, Arlington, TX 76013

800-489-0727 (toll free)

817-277-0727 (local)

817-277-2270 (fax)

E-mail: *info@fhautism.com*

www.fhautism.com

ISBN: 9780986067327

Acknowledgements

Many colleagues and friends were involved in the completion of this guidebook. It is with gratitude that we extend our thanks to the following people:

Leslie Larsen for sharing her ideas about activities that are useful in teaching relationship building and social interaction to youth with disabilities.

Marsha Shaw for her inspiration and collaboration in our early work.

Howard Mandeville and **Caroline Hoffman**, who supported us for many years through the Wisconsin Council on Developmental Disabilities.

Pat Patterson, who provided us with support and expert consultation for the many issues and concerns that we encounter with children with developmental disabilities, their families, and the people who support them.

The original production staff, including **Sabrina Ruland** and **Deborah Goldman** for layout, **Yvonne Slusser** for the cover graphics, and **Betsy Tru**e for the adult line drawings.

Future Horizons, Inc. for their support in editing and publishing the S·T·A·R·S guidebooks.

Illustrations were used for "Me and My World Scrapbook" with permission from *Let's Learn about Getting Along with Others*, by J. Carroll and illustrated by Elizabeth Nygaard, Good Apple, Inc., 1988.

We especially express our gratitude to all the youth and families who shared their experiences and stories with us: We have learned so much from you.

The Authors

Susan Heighway, M.S., PNP-BC, APNP, is a nurse practitioner with the University Center for Excellence in Developmental Disabilities at the Waisman Center and a faculty associate with the School of Nursing at the University of Wisconsin-Madison. At the Waisman Center, she works as a nurse practitioner in the outpatient specialty clinics serving individuals with developmental disabilities and metabolic and/or genetic disorders and their families. She is the nursing training coordinator for a federally funded maternal and child health interdisciplinary leadership training program for graduate students.

Susan Kidd Webster, MSSW, ISW, is Emeritus faculty of the School of Social Work at the University of Wisconsin-Madison. For many years, she worked on capacity-building projects as an outreach specialist with the Waisman Center to support people with developmental disabilities in the community. She taught courses and coordinated internships for undergraduate and graduate social work students working with persons with developmental disabilities. She is also the parent of an adult son with an intellectual disability.

Both Ms. Heighway and Ms. Webster have several years of experience in the area of sexual abuse prevention and sexuality education for people with developmental disabilities. For several years, they worked together at the Waisman Center. They both served on a task force that was convened by the Wisconsin Council on Developmental Disabilities and addressed issues of sexual abuse for people with developmental disabilities. They provided consultation to community agencies; presented at conferences; gave guest lectures on campus; and conducted workshops regarding sexuality and sexual abuse at the local, state, and national levels. They are the co-authors of the original S·T·A·R·S publication, which was published by Future Horizons, Inc., and was developed for adolescents and adults.

Contents

Introduction

This S·T·A·R·S 2 publication is an adapted version of our original S·T·A·R·S guidebook. S·T·A·R·S 2 is designed to be used with youth in the primary grades through high school. Our original S·T·A·R·S publication contains activities that were primarily designed for use in older teens and adults with developmental disabilities. As we met and talked about sexuality issues with parents, teachers, service providers, and persons with developmental disabilities, we became aware of the need for a corresponding training guide for children. We recognized that many of the problems in the area of sexuality and sexual abuse that adults with disabilities currently face could be lessened by early education and prevention.

The same comprehensive approach to sexuality education that was used in our original S·T·A·R·S guidebook is used in this book. This edition also focuses on the same four areas as the original S·T·A·R·S guidebook: **Understanding Relationships, Social Interaction, Sexual Awareness,** and **Assertiveness**. Goals and activities for each content area are included. Content and activities have been adapted for age appropriateness. Some areas have been expanded, and more emphasis is placed on creating and nurturing opportunities for normalized relationship building, socialization, and sexual expression.

Being part of an effort to help children understand and develop a positive sexuality and be safe from sexual abuse has many rewards. The children, teens, and adults who we have had the privilege of knowing have demonstrated the potential for significant growth in this area. We hope that this guidebook will be of practical benefit to others who are supporting and educating youth in this important area.

How to Use This Book

The Purpose
The purpose of this book is to share a model for promoting positive sexuality and preventing sexual abuse of youth. It is intended for use by parents, teachers, nurses and other health providers, counselors, sex therapists, social workers, psychologists, and others who are involved in teaching and supporting children and adolescents in this sensitive area.

The Activities

The activities in the guidebook are primarily designed for group work with grade school–aged children. This book is to be used as an instructional guide rather than a packaged curriculum, and instructors are encouraged to make adaptations to meet the individual needs of children. Users of the manual will need to figure out which activities are most suitable for participants. We also suggest that you enhance your training sessions with your own creative ideas. Suggestions for informal activities have also been included to assist in using the "teachable" moments that come up for youth and adults every day. The activities have been coded to designate age appropriateness and the complexity of information.

LOOK FOR THE FOLLOWING ACTIVITY CODES AT THE BOTTOM OF EACH PAGE IN THE FOUR CONTENT AREA SECTIONS:

☐ BASIC activities contain basic-level information.

■ ADVANCED activities contain more complex information and require an understanding of basic-level information.

☆ YOUNGER activities are suitable for children.

★ OLDER activities are suitable for adolescents and older teens.

Group or Individual

Most of the material in this book was developed from our work with groups, but we find that many of the activities and ideas are suited or easily adapted for individual training. Individual training may be preferred for some youths who do not learn well in a group or do not desire a group experience or when there are no resources available to support a group. For most youths, though, the advantages of participating in a group are significant. A group experience provides the opportunity for practicing social skills, peer modeling and coaching, as well as the opportunity to meet new people and make new friends.

Why Sexuality Education?

Sexuality is an important part of the total life experiences of all human beings. It should come as no surprise then that youth with developmental disabilities have sexual feelings, needs, and experiences. As with most people, their sexual desires are often linked with needs for closeness, caring, and emotional intimacy with others. Youth with developmental disabilities have unique learning needs in many aspects of their lives, and sexuality is no exception. Individualized guidance and education for promoting positive sexuality and the prevention of sexual abuse are essential.

Human sexuality encompasses a broad and complex spectrum of experiences and issues, including self-concept; sexual identity; sexual body functions; social interactions with the same or opposite sex; sexual expression, including masturbation and intercourse; sexual health; and future planning. For most of us, sexuality education has been haphazard at best, with some coming from our parents, much more coming from our peers, and the rest coming from one or two classes in school and messages of all kinds from the media.

For youth with disabilities, opportunities for gaining accurate knowledge about sexuality may be even more limited. Many youth with developmental disabilities don't have access to books, health classes, or the peer relationships where this knowledge can be easily obtained.

Parents, teachers, and others who support youth with disabilities may be unsure how much sexuality education to offer, or they may be embarrassed to talk about sexuality or not know how to do so. As a result, many youth with developmental disabilities lack basic sexual knowledge, are easily manipulated by others, and lack guidelines for the expression of sexual feelings.

It is important to teach youth with disabilities appropriate information about sexuality and sexual expression that fits their developmental needs. A comprehensive sexuality education program will give youth the opportunity to develop social skills necessary to engage in beneficial friendships and to adjust to their sexuality.

Sexuality education for youth with developmental disabilities contains the same information you would give to other typically developing children, but the content and manner in which it is presented may need to be adapted for the child's level of understanding and learning style.

By providing appropriate education, training, and support services in the area of sexuality and abuse prevention, it will be possible for youth with disabilities to acquire the skills and knowledge they need to develop a positive sexuality and reduce their risk for abuse.

Misbeliefs and Facts about Sexuality and Youth with Developmental Disabilities

Misbeliefs and misunderstandings about sexuality and people with disabilities can unnecessarily and drastically inhibit the sexual expression of people with disabilities. Misconceptions can also affect other areas of a person's life, including self-esteem, educational and vocational performance, and motivation to live as independently as possible. Misbeliefs need to be dispelled, and correct information must be provided.

Misbeliefs Regarding Sexuality

> ➤ Youth with developmental disabilities do not have sexual feelings or are asexual.

Or the other extreme:

> ➤ Youth with developmental disabilities are over-sexed and have uncontrollable urges.

> It is unnecessary to talk about sex and sexuality because youth with developmental disabilities won't understand it, be able to cope with it emotionally, or have the opportunity for sexual expression.

Facts Regarding Sexuality

Youth with developmental disabilities have a range of curiosity and awareness regarding sexuality similar to that of other young people.

The more accurate information and social skills training youth with disabilities receive, the more likely that their social and sexual behavior will be acceptable to community norms.

Misbeliefs Regarding Sexual Abuse

Children and teens with disabilities are not vulnerable to sexual assault because:

> People feel sorry for them or find them undesirable, so they will not be hurt.

> They spend their time in supervised or safe settings, so they are not exposed to dangerous or exploitative situations.

> They are not sexually active, so they are less vulnerable.

Facts Regarding Sexual Abuse

Children and teens with disabilities may be **more** vulnerable to sexual assault for several reasons:

> They may lack opportunities to acquire basic knowledge about anatomy, intercourse and other sexual activity (age appropriate), reproduction, and sexually transmitted diseases.

> They may lack information or education about sexual abuse.

> They may have been socialized to be compliant or passive and often have a strong desire to please.

> They may lack the opportunity to develop healthy social relationships.

> They may lack basic knowledge and understanding about how to safely use social media.

Section 2:
A S·T·A·R·S Model

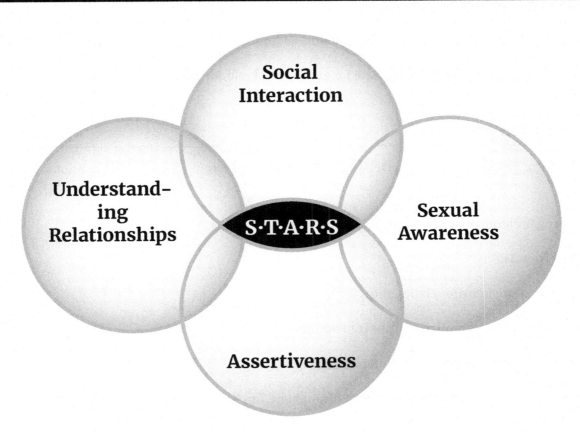

Social
Interaction

Understand–
ing
Relationships

S·T·A·R·S

Sexual
Awareness

Assertiveness

he S·T·A·R·S model originated through our efforts to design a training program for teaching basic personal safety skills to avoid sexual abuse. As we began working with individuals, we quickly learned that the issues of sexual abuse were connected to other issues, such as the person's self-esteem, assertiveness, understanding of sexuality, and opportunities to develop healthy relationships.

We recognized the need to teach and support positive expression of sexuality in addition to facilitating the learning of skills to prevent sexual abuse. Equally important were the environments in which people spent their time and the attitudes and values of family, teachers, caregivers, and the community at large. The realization of the complexity of the issues people were facing led us to develop our S·T·A·R·S model as a more comprehensive or holistic training model.

In our S·T·A·R·S model, we present a "building blocks" approach to training about the complex areas of sexuality and abuse prevention. Each content area offers concepts that are built upon in the next content area. For example, many of the activities in the "Assertiveness" section build upon content and behaviors that are acquired in all three of the previous content areas. The S·T·A·R·S model has four areas, with specific content areas in each:

Understanding Relationships

> Building a positive self-image.

> Identifying people in one's life as family, friends, acquaintances, community helpers, and strangers.

> Learning behaviors that are appropriate for each type of relationship.

Social Interaction

> Approaching, responding, and conversing with people in different settings and situations, including social media.

> Expressing preferences and making choices.

> Building friendships.

> Engaging in more mature relationships.

> Recognizing options for relationships into adulthood.

> Building a strong foundation for adult relationships.

> Understanding the responsibilities of parenthood and the pros and cons of having children.

Sexual Awareness

> Building a positive self-image and sexual identity.

> Identifying as male or female.

> Identifying body parts and understanding their functions.

> Understanding the difference between public and private behaviors.

> Differentiating between inappropriate and appropriate touching.

> Understanding the emotional and physical changes of puberty.

- Understanding sexual feelings and behaviors.

- Understanding reproduction.

- Examining societal norms and values regarding sexuality.

- Learning about sexually transmitted diseases.

- Discussing other health issues related to sexual awareness.

Assertiveness

- Increasing self-empowerment through words and actions, including responding to bullying.

- Recognizing a situation as potentially dangerous.

- Learning to say no and to use basic self-protection skills.

- Knowing how and where to get help at home, at school, and in the community.

- Reporting sexual exploitation or abuse.

Assessing the Needs of Children or "Figuring out What to Teach"

Parents and teachers often wonder when, what, and how they can teach a child with a disability about sexuality. While we believe it is essential to take the time to figure out what each youth needs to learn, we have not developed a specific "assessment tool" for children and youths in S·T·A·R·S 2. (Refer to the original S·T·A·R·S guidebook for two assessment tools—"The Sexual Attitudes and Knowledge Assessment" and the "Sexual Abuse Risks Assessment"—that are useful for older adolescents and adults with disabilities.)

We suggest that parents and teachers begin to approach the topic of sexuality for children with disabilities in a similar way it is approached for children without disabilities. One helpful resource is *How to Talk with Your Child About Sex: Help Your Children Develop a Positive Healthy Attitude Toward Sex and Relationships* by John Chirban, PhD, and published by Thomas Nelson, Inc. (2007). This book is a helpful resource regarding how and when to discuss sexuality, and it helps parents clarify their own thoughts and learn how to guide their children in developing the confidence, integrity, and honesty necessary for understanding sexuality.

Some pointers:

Support from others. Parents may want to get support from others when thinking about approaching sexuality with their child. Other parents of children with disabilities are often supportive. Asking the child's school teacher to become involved is helpful for many parents. The teacher and parents can share information on how the child best learns and ways of teaching that are successful. Making a plan together and reinforcing information between the two settings is very helpful. We encourage parents to advocate for the integration of goals in their child's individualized educational plan (IEP) regarding learning sexuality information, as well as social skills and assertiveness training.

Individualize for each child. Consider the child's chronologic age and figure out what information would be appropriate for any child of that age. Remember, the basics of sexuality begin at an early age (e.g., body parts and private and public concepts) and lay the groundwork for teaching throughout childhood and into adolescence. Materials and teaching methods must be individualized for the child's learning needs and abilities. Recognize that incongruities between the child's chronologic age, social maturity, and physical development may exist; this means that a youth who is 12 years old and going through puberty but whose cognitive abilities are more like those of a first grader will need the important information about body changes in puberty given in a manner that he or she will understand.

Consider:

What information and skills in the areas of sexual awareness, social skills, relationships, and assertiveness does the child already have?

What is the child's chronologic age? Social maturity? Cognitive ability?

What is the child's learning style?

What specific augmentative technologies (e.g., an iPad or voice output device) does the child use to communicate and learn?

What additional information and skills do you think the child needs to acquire?

Are there any specific concerns relating to sexuality that need to be addressed? Think about this in a comprehensive way; these are just a few concerns.

For example:

Does the child often get teased or bullied?

Has the child been prompted or exploited to do sexually inappropriate things?

Does the child tend to masturbate in inappropriate places (e.g., in front of people at home or at school)?

Has the child been sexually assaulted? Note that for this situation, specific counseling from a mental health counselor may be necessary in addition to teaching about sexuality.

Guidelines for Parents and Support Providers

Parents are generally considered the primary sexuality educators for their children. From the beginning, a child's sexuality is influenced by early family experiences, and guidance is received from caregivers. A family environment that supports the sexuality of the child in positive ways—such as through appropriate touching while bathing, dressing, and playing—leads to pleasure and pride in the child's body and an established sense of well-being. Positive early experiences provide the adolescent with a good basis for responding to changes during puberty.

In contrast, healthy sexual development may be impeded by discomfort with the subject of sex, negative comments about the child's body, uncertainty in the presentation of information, and fear regarding the adolescent's expression and control of sexual behavior. Children learn what they live. If they experience love and affection from caregivers who share it, then the sexuality they learn will be in the context of that love and affection. The experience of sexuality educators has shown that, when all is said and done, in general, the family still has the most powerful influence on the child.

Parents may not feel comfortable or knowledgeable in educating or responding to the child with respect to sexuality. Professionals, along with parents, may need to become more sensitive and participate in educational experiences that will increase comfort and knowledge about sexuality. Together, health professionals, educators, and parents can help youth build social competence and provide appropriate sexuality education that is respectful of family values.

When preparing to address sexuality with youth, these are things to do:

➤ Examine your own attitudes about sexuality in general and about sexuality and disability in particular. Foster a positive attitude about sexuality. The goal is to promote healthy sexuality and safety, not to eliminate sexual responses.

➤ Work toward becoming an "askable" adult regarding sexuality. This means that you listen carefully to everything a child says and avoid being overly judgmental. Children need to feel that they can ask questions without fear or punishment. At the same time, parents can seize these moments to reinforce and transmit their own family's values in a positive manner.

➤ Provide accurate information about sexuality. Even if a child never asks questions about sexuality, realize that the child has likely already acquired some information from other sources and needs to know that you will be there to clear up misconceptions, distortions, and fantasies. Provide straightforward, correct information, and check the child's understanding in a supportive manner.

➤ Recognize that telling your child about sex will not lead him or her to act out sexually. Instead, providing accurate information about sexual feelings and physical changes in clear-cut terms will reduce confusion and minimize the risk for inappropriate behavior.

> ➤ Be aware of the wide variety of behaviors, attitudes, values, and feelings related to sexuality, and deal with them in a sensitive manner.

Guidelines for Training

Group or Individual Learning

Most of the material in this book was developed from our work with groups, but we find that many of the activities and ideas are suited or easily adapted for individual training, as well. Individual training may be preferred for any youth who doesn't learn well in a group or doesn't want a group experience or when there are insufficient resources to support a group. For most youths, though, the advantages of participating in a group are great. The group provides opportunities for practicing social skills, peer modeling, and peer coaching, as well as meeting new people and making new friends.

Values Clarification

When teaching about human sexuality, it is important to discuss various family values or attitudes related to specific topics (e.g., masturbation, birth control, homosexuality, and abortion). It is important to give parents an opportunity to review instructional content and suggest at-home activities or discussions to teach their family's values. With youth, acknowledge the range of opinions and beliefs that exist, encouraging them to learn how their parents feel about such issues.

Inclusion of Sexuality Education Content in IEP

We encourage families to work with the school IEP team to incorporate appropriate goals and activities for promoting positive sexuality and preventing abuse in the school setting.

Working with a Group

Selecting Participants

Who?

S·T·A·R·S 2 activities were developed for youth with autism or other developmental disabilities. Children, from preschool age to adolescents in high school, can benefit from its content. We also believe that the information presented here is valuable to all children and could be effectively used in settings in which children both with and without disabilities are learning together.

Co-ed or not?

Groups can be co-educational or organized separately for girls and boys. We have found that co-ed groups emulate the "real world." Such groups enhance role-playing and other activities and foster an appreciation for human development and sexuality issues in both sexes. The content area and/or the comfort level of the instructor may influence whether the instruction is done for a co-ed group or not. If the adult facilitator is comfortable, even gender-sensitive issues, such as menstruation and condom use, can be taught and discussed in a co-ed group. Sometimes, girls and boys may feel more comfortable learning some content separately. For example, we believe that both girls and boys can benefit from learning about and seeing menstrual hygiene products; however, some of the more explicit discussion and demonstration about their use may best be done with girls only. For each area, use your judgment about what will work best for you and your participants.

Number of Youths in the Group

We recommend that the size of the group be small (four to eight youths). Size will depend on the individual needs of the participants, participants' learning styles, and the capacity of group leaders.

Number and Frequency of Teaching Sessions

Information should be shared at a pace that is comfortable for the group or individual. The pace will vary with the age and learning style of the youths. For children, having sessions at least two times per week usually works well for continuity of content.

Involvement of Parents

Whenever there is instruction on human sexuality for minor children and youths, it is best to involve parents or guardians at the outset. If you are offering sexuality education as part of a school human growth and development curriculum, become familiar with the guidelines, which were established by the school board for your school district regarding parent or guardian involvement. A sample parent letter is included in the Appendix (page A-3).

Some instructors offer to meet with parents individually or as a group to review content. This not only informs parents about the content of the training but can promote continuity and reinforcement of the training at home. Sometimes, a parent group meets concurrently with the youth group to clarify and discuss content and concerns that are pertinent to sexuality.

Instructional Methods

In general, information that will be presented to youth with disabilities will be the same as that for other youth, except it is presented in simpler words, at a slower pace, and with much repetition. Any information that you share with an individual child must be presented with methods that are best for teaching that child. For example, it may be helpful to break the content down into the simplest concepts; use simple language; or use visual aids, such as pictures, drawings, or a Social Stories™ format.

We suggest that a variety of instructional methods be used, such as individual and group instruction, simple workbook activities, art, songs and games, puppets, "Social Stories™," and role-playing. Anatomic dolls, photographs, and line drawings are the most effective methods for identifying reproductive body parts. Group discussion and question and answer sessions are the most effective techniques for problem solving. Social skills are best taught through "real life practice," role-playing, and group discussion. Lecturing is the least effective method because participants may lose interest if they are not actively engaged.

For some activities, we may refer to specific resources (e.g., slides). Effective teaching can happen even if you don't have access to the latest technology. Some of the best teaching tools are creatively made with common materials and are tailored to the individual child.

Me and My World Scrapbook

Pages of this scrapbook are located in the Appendix and can be copied for each child. The materials can be adapted for a child of any age with age-appropriate stickers or artwork. There are specific suggestions for using the scrapbook in the "Activities" sections. When completed, youth can keep it as a scrapbook about themselves. The scrapbook can be periodically reviewed with youth, either formally or informally, to reinforce concepts that were learned in the group format.

Role-playing

Role-playing is a particularly effective technique because it involves the active participation of children, giving them an opportunity to try out and rehearse new behaviors and identify and change inappropriate behaviors. Peer feedback and coaching give the youth who observe the role-play exercise an opportunity to learn the concepts by asking them to judge and identify the strengths and needs of the role players.

A potential drawback of role-playing is that, at times, it can become too "real" for some children. For example, when someone is acting out a situation in which he or she is angry, a participant may believe that the person really is angry. And when role-playing a threatening situation, a participant may become truly frightened. It is important to keep reminding role players that it is only make-believe. Another drawback is that role players may get too caught up in the fun of role-playing and work at being good actors rather than focus on learning the concepts being taught.

Activities in the Natural Setting

Children and youth benefit most from this program when time is spent reviewing content and practicing skills related to the sexuality education training program in their natural settings. If trainers are not available for this individual work, other persons in the participant's support network could carry out this training activity. This time can be used to practice and reinforce skills and knowledge covered in the group meeting and focus on is-sues identified for each child. At the end of the "Activities" section for each of the four content areas, an "Informal Activities" section is included.

Circle of Friends

All children benefit from having friends and being part of a social group. Children with disabilities often need the same level of direction and support in making friends as they do in other areas of their lives. We are learning more about individuals with autism spectrum disorder and their common human desire for friendships; that is, even though they may not appear interested in others, they have a desire for social connections. "Circles of Friends" is one way of expanding and enhancing friendships for children.

How it works:

1. Make a list of peers without disabilities with whom the focus child has contact during the day. Contact may occur in mainstreamed classes, peer tutoring, recreation or sports, passing from class to class, recess, or lunch. Peers can be identified through observation; by asking the focus child; and by talking with teachers, classroom aids, or other school personnel.

2. Note the quality of interactions, and identify a shorter list of potential friends. Try to include one or two peers with whom the focus child may have shared interests, such as music, art, computers, video games, and sports. Social media, when used with safeguards, can be a useful tool for organizing a Circle of Friends.

3. Talk to each of the potential peers about Circle of Friends. Explain that its purpose is to help the focus child make friends and feel more connected with school.

4. Select the peer or peers who demonstrate the greatest interest in being involved for inclusion in the Circle.

5. Ask the peer or peers to identify three to five of their friends who might know the focus child or who might be interested in joining the group.

6. Invite four to six peers to an introductory meeting. Collect more information about the youths' schedules, daily routines, and interests. Brainstorm possible activities and outings.

7. Circles usually meet about once a week for about an hour, but the frequency and length of the meetings depend on the age of the kids, the setting, the kids' schedules, etc. Kids initially meet for group activities, but as the focus child develops friendships with the other peers, encourage one-on-one or smaller group experiences. Think of times during the day when pairing is possible. At first, the group may want to make a schedule or calendar mapping out interaction times. See samples below.

8. Over time, the adult should fade from the social group as much as possible to allow typical interactions and

friendships to more naturally occur. It is important to remain available for problem solving, conflict resolution, and other kinds of support as needed.

9. If Circle of Friends activities are to take place in settings other than school, which we highly recommend, parents will also need to be involved (e.g., for transportation). It is a good idea to notify parents that their child is participating in Circle of Friends, invite their encouragement and support, and respond to any concerns.

Excerpted and revised from "Setting Up and Managing Peer Support Networks: Social Context Research Project—Methods for Facilitating the Inclusion of Students with Disabilities," In *Integrated School and Community Context*, edited by C. Green, C. Kennedy, and T. Haring, University of California, Santa Barbara.

Sample Schedule for Circle of Friends

Schedule for one-on-one or smaller group interaction with Michelle outside of class

When	Who	Where
Before school	Jenny	Side playground
Between 2nd & 3rd periods	Ann	Room 302
Lunch	Lisa, John	Lunchroom
Recess	Lisa, Jenny	Rear playground
Between 5th & 6th periods	Kim	Michelle's locker

Sample Calendar for Circle of Friends

OCTOBER

Monday	Tuesday	Wednesday	Thursday	Friday	Saturday
		1 **2:15 Circle Group**	2 **4:00 East Towne Mall (Lisa & Michelle)**	3	4
6	7	8 **2:15 Circle Group**	9	10	11 **11:00 Roller Skate Party**
13	14 **7:00 PM Basketball Game (Jenny & Mi- chelle)**	15 **2:15 Circle Group**	16	17	18
20	21	22 **2:15 Circle Group**	23	24 **Sleepover at Kim's**	25
27	28	29 **2:15 Circle Group**	30	31 **Halloween**	

Section 3:
Understanding Relationships

Except for the hermit on the mountain, most of us live our daily lives in a network of relationships. Societal trends—such as population mobility, social media, blended families, alternate child care arrangements, and the inclusion of children with disabilities in settings with children who do not have disabilities—have increased the variety of people with whom children relate. Children's understanding of the various types of relationships in their network directs and influences their interactions and behaviors. The ability to identify people as family members, intimate and close friends, acquaintances, community helpers, and strangers is a key component for children to build satisfying relationships and protect themselves from abusive situations. This is especially important with the growth of social media. Many youth need direct instruction to understand the various kinds of relationships and the norms for behavior and social interaction that are appropriate for each social setting.

When focusing on relationship building, the focus of our efforts must not be solely on teaching children to understand existing relationships, but, perhaps more importantly, on creating and providing opportunities for meaningful relationships to happen and grow. With trends toward more inclusion and integration, children and youth with disabilities have the potential to expand their relationship network. On the other hand, if children are not assisted in developing relationships in integrated settings, they may be even more isolated. We have included resources on developing a "Circle of Friends" as one way of developing and nurturing friendships.

Having positive relationships is at the core of our feelings of well-being. Supporting relationships may be the most important investment we make toward improving the quality of life for children with developmental disabilities.

Goal 1: Building a Positive Self–Image

Activities:

1. 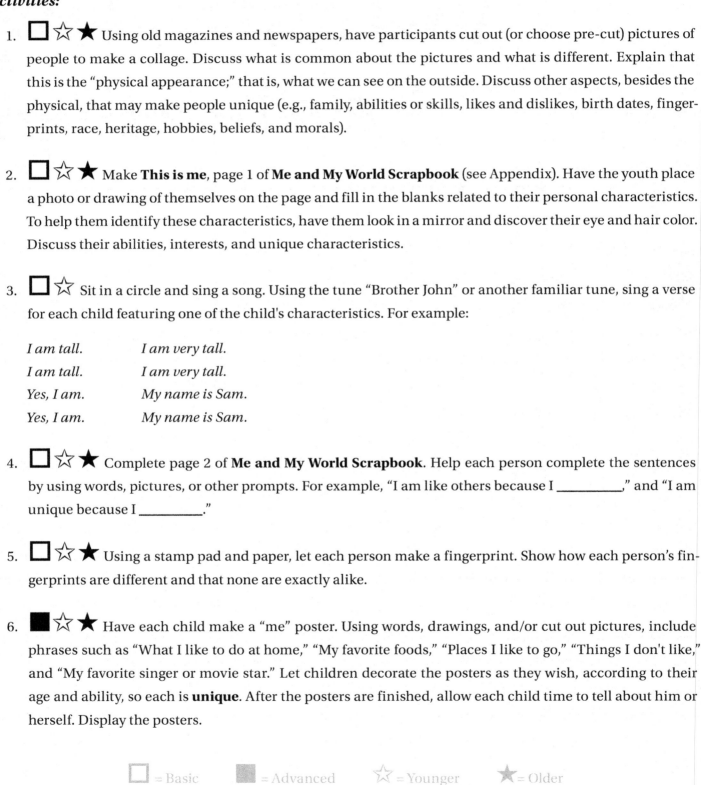 Using old magazines and newspapers, have participants cut out (or choose pre-cut) pictures of people to make a collage. Discuss what is common about the pictures and what is different. Explain that this is the "physical appearance;" that is, what we can see on the outside. Discuss other aspects, besides the physical, that may make people unique (e.g., family, abilities or skills, likes and dislikes, birth dates, finger-prints, race, heritage, hobbies, beliefs, and morals).

2. Make **This is me**, page 1 of **Me and My World Scrapbook** (see Appendix). Have the youth place a photo or drawing of themselves on the page and fill in the blanks related to their personal characteristics. To help them identify these characteristics, have them look in a mirror and discover their eye and hair color. Discuss their abilities, interests, and unique characteristics.

3. Sit in a circle and sing a song. Using the tune "Brother John" or another familiar tune, sing a verse for each child featuring one of the child's characteristics. For example:

   I am tall.   *I am very tall.*
   I am tall.   *I am very tall.*
   Yes, I am.   *My name is Sam.*
   Yes, I am.   *My name is Sam.*

4. Complete page 2 of **Me and My World Scrapbook**. Help each person complete the sentences by using words, pictures, or other prompts. For example, "I am like others because I _____," and "I am unique because I _____."

5. Using a stamp pad and paper, let each person make a fingerprint. Show how each person's fin-gerprints are different and that none are exactly alike.

6. Have each child make a "me" poster. Using words, drawings, and/or cut out pictures, include phrases such as "What I like to do at home," "My favorite foods," "Places I like to go," "Things I don't like," and "My favorite singer or movie star." Let children decorate the posters as they wish, according to their age and ability, so each is **unique**. After the posters are finished, allow each child time to tell about him or herself. Display the posters.

☐ = Basic   ■ = Advanced   ☆ = Younger   ★ = Older

7. ■☆★ Complete **My Favorite Things**, page 3 of **Me and My World Scrapbook**.

8. ■☆★ Have children think about when they are proud of or pleased with themselves. Complete **I Am Proud**, page 4 of **Me and My World Scrapbook** ("I am proud of myself when _____.").

9. ■☆★ Share with youth that how we feel about ourselves involves both things we can see on the "outside" and things in our mind, or "inside." List things we can see on the **outside** (our physical appearance) and things in our mind, on the **inside** (our beliefs and feelings).

10. ■☆★ Make a booklet in the shape of a male or female with lines for writing. On the front, or "outside," have students list the things that people can **see** that they like about themselves (their physical self). On the "inside" of the book, list things they like about themselves that can't be seen (their emotional self [e.g., cheerful, honest, helpful, friendly]).

11. ■☆★ Complete **When I'm Grown Up**, page 5 of **Me and My World Scrapbook**. It is important for youth with disabilities to have a positive vision of themselves in the future. Help youth share their pages with each other.

12. □■☆★ Invite adults with intellectual, physical, sensory or other challenges to share their achievements with participants.

13. □■☆★ Have participants sit in a circle and take turns saying something they like about the person sitting next to them. This gives youth practice affirming others, as well as receiving affirmation.

14. □■☆★ Use puppets (for younger children) or role-plays (for older children) to demonstrate situations in which people give and receive compliments. Include examples of complimenting appearance ("What a cool haircut!"), behavior ("I like the way you are sitting quietly."), and completion of an effort or task ("Look what a great job you've done!"). Be certain to practice and generalize this skill in school and community environments.

Informal Activities:

1. □■☆★ There are many opportunities to foster self-esteem on a daily basis in natural settings. Making positive statements like, "John, I'm so glad to see you today." or "I'd like to show everyone how beautiful Sarah's writing is." helps enhance a child's self-esteem.

□ = Basic   ■ = Advanced   ☆ = Younger   ★ = Older

2. ☐ ■ ☆ ★ Peer groups can learn to reinforce each other. For example, clapping for each other's successes and making comments to each other using "I like _____" statements helps develop this skill.

3. ☐ ■ ☆ ★ Create and recognize opportunities for children to share their accomplishments (e.g., verbalize, sign, gesture, or use pictures).

Goal 2: Identifying People in One's Life as Family, Friends, Acquaintances, Community Helpers, and Strangers

Before beginning this section, you can send a letter to the child's parent or guardian requesting information about the child's network of relationships. (See the Appendix for a sample letter to a parent or guardian about relationships.) If the child is older and able to provide the requested information, the letter may not be necessary, although it helps share content about this training program with significant others so that they can reinforce concepts and express any concerns.

Activities:

1. ☐ ☆ ★ Talk about "What is a family?" Discuss all types of families (e.g., two-parent, single-parent, foster, and grandparents raising children).   `FAMILY`

2. ☐ ☆ ★ Read age-appropriate children's books and/or look at pictures from magazines about families and family activities. TV provides lots of examples, too.

3. ☐ ☆ ★ Have youth share family photos and identify by name or point to members of their family. Place photos, drawings, or names of family members on **My Family**, page 6 of **Me and My World Scrapbook**.

4. ☐ ☆ ★ Discuss extended family members: grandparents, aunts, uncles, and cousins. Add other significant family members to **My Family**, page 6 of **Me and My World Scrapbook**.

5. ☐ ■ ☆ ★ Have youth make a family tree by using the **Family Tree** on pages 7 and 8 of **Me and My World Scrapbook**. Trees can depict the child's current family or household. On a more advanced level, trace the youth's roots.

6. ☐ ■ ☆ ★ Complete **Who Lives In My House**, page 9 of **Me and My World Scrapbook**. Some children

☐ = Basic　　■ = Advanced　　☆ = Younger　　★ = Older

may need two houses (e.g., those with divorced parents or who are in foster care). Some households may include persons who are not relatives. Talk about these relationships.

7. ☐ ■ ☆ ★ Group discussion: "Who are your friends?" and "What is a friend?" Ask participants to name a friend and tell why that person is a friend. On a wall poster, list reasons why we call people "friends." Try to elicit responses such as: fun to play with, care about my feelings (and vice versa), go places together, and help each other. The focus here is to understand who our friends are and what friendship means. See the section entitled "Social Interaction" for activities related to how to make and socialize with friends.

This is a good time to discuss social media, including both positive opportunities for meeting new friends and the potentially negative and scary aspects of connecting with harmful individuals. See the section entitled "Resources" for more detailed references and guidance in this area.

8. ☐ ☆ Have children make a paper doll chain (or hand out pre-cut chains) with names of their friends on it.

9. ■ ☆ ★ Discuss other aspects of friendship. Points to emphasize:

   › The difference between a close friend and a casual friend.

   › Friendships often take time to develop. Have children discuss any long-time friends that they have.

   › Friends may not get along every day.

   › Friends change, and it is ok to stop being friends if a relationship doesn't make you feel good.

10. ■ ☆ ★ Complete **My Friends**, page 10 of **Me and My World Scrapbook**. Younger kids can paste on paper doll chain friends. Older kids can have their friends autograph the page or write the names of their friends in a friendship circle.

11. ■ ☆ ★ Use puppets or role-plays to demonstrate examples of being a friend and not being a friend. For example, show a person:

    › Inviting another to join an activity.

    › Excluding another from play.

☐ = Basic   ■ = Advanced   ☆ = Younger   ★ = Older

➤ Helping someone.

➤ Sharing toys or candy.

➤ Grabbing someone's toy or taking someone's belongings.

➤ Saying something nice to someone.

➤ Bullying, teasing, or calling someone a name.

Have children talk about which behaviors caused good feelings and which ones caused bad feelings.

12. ■ ☆ ★ Another type of relationship you may want to include here is "romantic" relationships Explain that teenagers and adults sometimes have friendships that develop into romantic relationships, such as between a husband and wife or two people who are dating. In a romantic relationship, a person has special feelings for someone else. These feelings are called "being in love." Ask the children or teens if they know people who are "in love." See the sections entitled "Social Interaction" and "Sexual Awareness" for further discussion of romantic relationships.

ROMANTIC RELATIONSHIPS

13. □ ☆ ★ Define "acquaintances": people whose names we know or recognize but who are not as close to us as family or friends. Examples might include: some neighbors, the school janitor, some students at school, some co-workers at your job or where your parents work, and a familiar store clerk.

ACQUAINTANCES

14. □ ☆ ★ Complete **Acquaintances**, page 11 of **Me and My World Scrapbook**, which helps children iden-tify acquaintances in a variety of settings.

15. □ ☆ ★ Talk about strangers. Define a stranger as anyone you do not know and whose name you do not know.

STRANGERS

16. ■ ☆ ★ Help children identify who is and is not a stranger. Ask children to differentiate people they know from those they don't know by naming specific friends, family members, and acquaintances, as well as strangers. For example, "Is the woman walking down the street a stranger? Is the garbage collector a stranger? Is the school librarian a stranger?" Review why people are or are not strangers.

17. ■ ☆ ★ Discuss types of strangers (people who you do not know and whose names you do not know).

□ = Basic   ■ = Advanced   ☆ = Younger   ★ = Older

Safe strangers. These include: (a) community helpers, such as police, fire fighters, mail carriers, health care workers, and people you could ask for help in an emergency, and (b) other people who live in the community, such as sales clerks, restaurant workers, other shoppers, and people at the bus stop. Some of these people you could also ask for help.

Make **Community Helpers**, page 12 of **Me and My World Scrapbook**.

Dangerous strangers. These include people who want to harm others and from whom you want to protect yourself.

Help children identify possible clues that someone may be a dangerous stranger. Make a chart with examples, including:

> Someone you do not know who asks you to go somewhere with him or her or to get into his or her car.

> Someone who offers to give you money or a present if you do something that doesn't seem right.

> Someone who threatens to hurt you if you "tell."

> Someone who approaches you over the Internet and asks for personal information or to meet you somewhere.

18. ■ ☆ ★ Help children use their intuition or "gut feelings" to identify possible dangerous strangers or unsafe situations. Discuss how your body feels when you are afraid or scared (e.g., stomachache, heart pounding, breathing quickly, and sweaty hands). This means that your body is telling you that something isn't quite right. Children should learn to respond to these feelings. Tell them not to talk to the person, to get away from that person, and to tell a safe person about the encounter. Protective behavior skills are more fully discussed in the section entitled "Assertiveness."

19. ■ ☆ ★ Emphasize that most strangers will not harm you and that you can use the clues discussed above and your "gut" feelings to help you tell if someone is dangerous.

20. ☐ ☆ ★ We suggest using a relationship concentric circle mapping tool (such as the CIRCLES program) for teaching about social relationships, rules, and behavior. It is a helpful teaching tool designed to help youth who have difficulty learning the abstract concepts of personal space, social distance, and appropriate social and sexual behavior. It can be used to teach social distance and levels of familiarity through

 = Basic   = Advanced   ☆ = Younger   ★ = Older

the use of concentric circles. We recommend using the tool in all settings in which students spend time to practice positive social behaviors that are specific for each setting. Learning positive social behaviors helps students be successful in social interactions with others, decrease vulnerability, and prevent sexual abuse.

Give each participant a paper with concentric circles identifying the different types of relationships (e.g., private or personal, family, friends, community helpers, and strangers). Some participants may benefit from using photos or names to identify people in their life. (See the example below of a relationship concentric circles mapping tool.)

Strangers

Community Helpers

Friends

Best Friends

Family

Private

Relationship Concentric Circles Mapping Tool

Informal Activities:

1. ■ ☆ ★ Throughout the day, ask children to label people as an acquaintance, friend, or stranger. For example, after the mail carrier delivers the mail, ask if he or she is an acquaintance, friend, or stranger.

2. ■ ☆ ★ When in the community (e.g., at the shopping mall, park, or downtown), have children identify community helpers and generally "safe" strangers such as clerks, adults with other children, bus drivers, and police. If possible, point out potentially unsafe people to avoid, such as those who appear intoxicated and people who are fighting.

Goal 3: Learning Appropriate Behaviors for Each Type of Relationship

This section teaches the basics of general norms of social interaction. In the next section, participants will learn to further differentiate interactions based on things such as place, situation, and nonverbal cues from others.

GREETING OTHERS

Activities:

1. ☐ ☆ ★ **Who Would You ...?** Make a poster with headings for the following behaviors: Kiss, Hug, Shake Hands, Hi-Five, Fist Bump, Smile, Wave, Don't Talk To, and Say NO! Under each behavior, have participants list the people with whom it would be alright to interact in these ways.

   ■ ☆ ★ On a more advanced level, review these concepts in a discussion.

RELATING ACTIONS TO RELATIONSHIPS

2. ■ ☆ ★ **"Is It OK?"** game. Read aloud the questions below about social behavior. Have participants respond to the questions by holding up a card that says "OK" or "NOT OK" (or "YES" or "NO").

   ➤ Is it ok to kiss the store clerk?

   ➤ Is it ok to hug your mother?

   ➤ Is it ok to hug the mail carrier?

   ➤ Is it ok to kiss someone you just met?

> Is it ok to wave to your coach?

■ ☆ ★ On an advanced level, review these concepts in a discussion. Acknowledge that behavior sometimes depends on circumstances such as where and when the interaction is taking place.

3. ■ ☆ ★ Use puppets or role-plays to help youth learn behaviors that are generally appropriate with different relationships. For example:

> Meeting a friend of your dad's.

> Coming home from school and greeting your mom.

> Saying goodbye to a good friend.

> Meeting a neighbor for the first time.

> Meeting a new classmate.

> Seeing your teacher at a restaurant.

> Welcoming relatives to your home.

4. ☐ ☆ ★ Using completed pages 6, 10, 11, and 12 of **Me and My World Scrapbook**, have participants affix the greeting stickers from page 16 of the scrapbook to the appropriate people or relationship. For example, place the kiss or hug sticker on sister, Sara; the wave sticker on neighbor, Jim; and the smile sticker on principal, Mrs. Davis.

5. ■ ☆ ★ Using CIRCLES (a relationship concentric circles mapping tool) or a similar visual tool, review the levels of intimacy between people and pair them with socially appropriate behaviors for those relationships.

Give each participant a separate piece of paper with concentric circles. Go through each type of relationship and the appropriate behaviors for that relationship. Individually or in a group, address questions about each level of intimacy. (For the visual tool, refer to Goal 2, Activity 20, in the section entitled "Understanding Relationships.")

☐ = Basic   ■ = Advanced   ☆ = Younger   ★ = Older

Section 4:
Social Interaction

The opportunity for social interaction is important to all of us. To effectively interact, we acquire social skills. We learn how to approach and respond to people in ways that are acceptable for our culture. As we are socialized, we learn to express our needs, preferences, and opinions; how to give and receive information; and how to make friends and develop close relationships.

As persons with developmental or other differences become more involved in community life, we realize that the need for social skill training is as important as instruction in cooking, money management, housekeeping, and shopping. Social skills are often acknowledged as important, yet they are given low priority when individual learning goals are written and carried out. As a result, many youth lack the skills to effectively communicate their feelings and wishes and relate to others without guidance and support. Some youth may even develop inappropriate or antisocial behaviors that jeopardize their participation in educational and vocational programs. Direct instruction in social skills, positive role modeling, and lots of opportunity for practice can greatly enhance social integration of youth. In addition, often the actions or behavioral characteristics of youth with autism may be misinterpreted by others who don't understand those behaviors. Efforts to enhance social interaction should also be directed at helping others accept the youth's behavior or verbalizations.

Along with training, our energies should be directed at creating natural opportunities for children and youth to develop and practice social skills. Spending hours teaching a child how to "make a friend" is futile if, in reality, the youth has little opportunity to meet, play with, or learn with his or her peers.

Social adjustment is also closely linked to self-esteem. Years of isolation, limited participation in community life, and feelings of failure have left many adults with poor self-concepts and difficulty relating to others. With this generation, we think there is much we can do to prevent and counteract the ill effects of labels and limited opportunities. It begins with helping young people see themselves as attractive human beings, appreciate their gifts and talents, and develop a positive vision of themselves in the future. Thus, many of the activities in this section promote a positive self-concept.

A person's self-concept is also enhanced by opportunities to make choices, express preferences, and give opinions. Social skills development in this area is excellent groundwork for a later section entitle "Assertiveness."

Some teens also need support and "coaching" about romantic relationships. We think it is one of the most important ways we can help people develop satisfying relationships and decrease their vulnerability to sexual abuse.

Goal 1: Approaching, Responding, and Conversing with People in Different Settings and Situations

This section builds on knowledge gained in the section entitled "Understanding Relationships." Participants will learn that interactions are not only influenced by **who** is interacting but also **where** and **when** the interaction is taking place.

Activities:

1. ☐ ☆ ★ **Who and where would you ...?** On a large sheet of paper, write the word MOTHER or someone you may kiss. Then list several settings (e.g., home, the grocery store, a ball game, and a restaurant). Ask if it is acceptable to kiss in all of these places and what other factors might be important (e.g., your age, the presence of others, the type of activity going on). Continue the activity for other people, behaviors, and settings.

   RELATING ACTIONS TO SETTINGS

   ■ ☆ ★ On a more advanced level, discuss how behaviors or interactions differ according to the setting, as well as the person.

2. ■ ☆ **Can I Do This Here?** Create a game with a board and a set of cards. On the game board, use pictures or words of various locations or environments in which children spend time, such as their home (including the living room, bedroom, bathroom, and kitchen), school (including the hall, classroom, restroom, and playground), the bus, the street, a bowling alley, church, a movie theater, the park, a doctor's office, a restaurant, a grocery store, and a work place.

   Prepare a set of cards, each of which represent a behavior such as kissing Mom, talking loudly, going with a stranger, taking off your clothes, "cuddling" with a girlfriend or boyfriend, and hugging your best friend. Take turns drawing a card from the pile and determining which places on the game board this behavior would be appropriate. Points or chips can be earned for each correct answer. Discuss the various choices that players make. This concept may also be taught and practiced through discussion and application in community settings.

☐ = Basic   ■ = Advanced   ☆ = Younger   ★ = Older

3. ☐ ☆ ★ Identify facial expressions and feelings. Show children various facial expressions and label the feelings that go along with them (e.g., angry, sad, and happy). Have the children make the facial expressions, as well. It helps to use a mirror.

EXPRESSING & RECOGNIZING FEELINGS

4. ■ ☆ ★ Play the **What Does The Face Say?** game. Using the sample faces in the Appendix (page A-X), label facial expressions (e.g., angry, sad, surprised, happy, frightened, and tired). To play, have a child select a facial expression and imitate it, and then have classmates guess the feeling that it expresses.

5. ■ ☆ ★ Role-play the expression of various feelings by using words, signs, pictures, gestures, or expressions. Adapt the activity depending on the age level.

For example, how would you express:

> Friendliness?

> Love?

> Anger?

> Feeling sorry?

NOTE: Sometimes those who have cerebral palsy or similar disabilities that affect muscle movement have difficulty making their facial expression match their emotion. If you are working with someone for whom this is a challenge, be sensitive to the possible frustration they may experience communicating feelings, and assist them in developing alternate ways of communicating their emotions. If you are helping someone develop a sign board or alternate communication system, be sure to include symbols or pictures for feelings and emotions.

6. ☐ ☆ Sit in a circle and make up verses about feelings to the tune of "Brother John" or another familiar tune. For example:

I am tall.	*I am very tall.*
I am tall.	*I am very tall.*
Yes, I am.	*My name is Sam.*
Yes, I am.	*My name is Sam.*

7. ■ ☆ ★ **What Is The Message?** Role-play situations in which children are asked to decipher nonverbal communications.

☐ = Basic   ■ = Advanced   ☆ = Younger   ★ = Older

For example, what is the message if someone:

➤ Smiles and nods her head? (Yes or ok.)

➤ Extends an arm and hand when greeting? (Wants to shake hands.)

➤ Pulls his body back when approached for hug? (Doesn't want to hug.)

➤ Shakes head back and forth? (No or not ok.)

8. ☐ ☆ ★ Introduce the concepts of privacy and private. Include these points:

➤ Sometimes we all have the right to be alone (i.e., privacy).

➤ Your body belongs to you.

➤ Your body has private parts.

➤ In most cases, no one should touch you unless you want to be touched.

➤ You should not touch another person unless he or she wants to be touched.

9. ☐ ☆ ★ Help participants identify "private" places, such as at home (a bedroom or bathroom) and at school (a cubby or locker, desk, or bathroom). Complete **My Private Spaces** and **My Private Things**, page 13 of **Me and My World Scrapbook**. Talk about the importance of each person respecting the privacy of others. Participants may want to make or have a "PRIVATE" sign to use.

10. ☐ ☆ ★ Talk about the concept that parts of our bodies are also private. You may simplify this concept by saying the parts that your underwear or bathing suit cover are your private parts and include your buttocks, genital area, and breasts.

Discuss which parts of our bodies are considered "private" while emphasizing any part that you don't **want** touched is private **to you!** (Correct anatomic labeling is covered later, in the section entitled "Sexual Awareness." At this point, it is not the major objective.)

11. ☐ ☆ ★ Provide youth with a line drawing of male and female children (pages 18–22 of the Appendix). For each individual, decide whether it is appropriate to only use the line drawings of the pre-pubertal youth or whether to also use the line drawing of the fully developed adult. Have students draw or paste a picture of a bathing suit onto the drawing to cover the private parts. If available, anatomically correct dolls are also great for demonstrating this concept.

☐ = Basic   ▪ = Advanced   ☆ = Younger   ★ = Older

12. ☐ ■ ☆ ★ Discuss the fact that some people need help with bathing and toileting, which **may** require caregivers to touch private parts. Explain to all children that sometimes a parent, nurse, or physician may need to look at or touch a private part if the child is sick or hurt. Say that this is different from "sexual" touching, which will be more fully discussed in the section entitled "Sexual Awareness."

☐ ■ ☆ ★ If appropriate, discuss the bathing and toileting exceptions individually with the participant and help him or her identify his or her own needs.

13. ☐ ■ ☆ ★ Emphasize that people do not touch each other's private parts except for very intimate relationships, such as between a husband and wife and when medical or personal care is needed.

Informal Activities:

1. ■ ☆ ★ When watching TV programs or movies, discuss relationships and interactions in the story. For example, "The teenagers are friends. How can we tell?" Point out examples of both positive and negative interactions. "See how they care about each other?" or "They are being rude to the waitress."

2. ■ ☆ ★ When in community settings such as shopping malls and the zoo, use the opportunity to quietly identify relationships and behaviors of people you see.

3. ☐ ■ ☆ ★ Throughout the day, look for opportunities to reinforce positive interactions on the part of the participant. Gently correct inappropriate behaviors. For example, "I don't want to kiss you, but I would like to hold your hand." Remember to teach or model the desired behavior rather than reprimanding the child for inappropriate behavior.

4. ☐ ■ ☆ ★ If the child engages in a "private" activity (e.g., masturbation) in a non-private or public place, interrupt the behavior and give information about if, when, and where the behavior is ok. Then redirect the child to another activity. Try to "teach" rather than scold.

5. ☐ ■ ☆ ★ Provide as many opportunities as possible for participants to interact with others in daily life, including people both with and without disabilities. Use cuing, prompting, and modeling to support skill development as needed.

6. ☐ ■ ☆ ★ Utilize relevant computer software and applications to teach social skills. Refer to the section entitled "Resources" for references.

☐ = Basic　　■ = Advanced　　☆ = Younger　　★ = Older

Goal 2: Expressing Preferences, Making Choices

Often, children have very limited opportunities for choice making. As a result, they grow up relying on others' judgment of what is best for them. Learning to express their preferences, opinions, and wishes will help them develop skills of assertion, which are needed to prevent abuse, and an understanding of the importance of their own needs and integrity.

Activities:

1. ☐ ■ ☆ ★ Provide opportunities for choice making in both structured and un-
   structured activities. For example, "Who wants to be on the blue team?" "What color
   marker do you want to use?" "Choose a seat in the circle." "Who wants to be in the
   role-play?" Start with simple choice making and gradually encourage more compli-
   cated decision making (e.g., "What would you do in this situation?").

   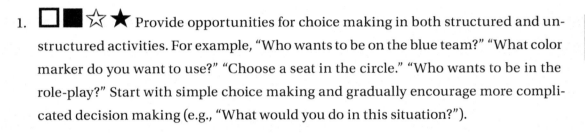

   EXPRESSING PREFERENCE

2. ☐ ☆ ★ Review or repeat **My Favorite Things**, from the section entitled "Understanding Relationships," Goal 1, activity 7.

3. ☐ ☆ ★ Show two or three pieces of artwork, and ask each person which one he or she likes the most and why.

   ■ ☆ ★ On a more advanced level, discuss individual preferences or tastes. Ask what opportunities people have to make choices (e.g., clothes, room decor, and activities). Explain that choices usually expand as we get older.

4. ■ ☆ ★ Provide scenarios (short stories) in which the character must make a choice. Have students choose what they would do and why.

   MAKING DECI-SIONS

   Examples of short stories:

   ➤ Sue's parents have decided to paint her bedroom. She can choose to have it painted blue, pink, or yellow. What do you think would look nice?

   ➤ Mike's class is going on a picnic. What do you think would be good to bring along to eat?

   ➤ Kim's Brownie troop is going on a field trip. Where do you think it would be fun to go? Should they go to a museum, the zoo, or the beach?

☐ = Basic   ■ = Advanced   ☆ = Younger   ★ = Older

➤ Your teacher tells you about a new club that is forming after school that you could join. Discuss the things you might want to consider when making your decision (e.g., what activities will be going on, who will be there, and if it takes place at a convenient time).

➤ The kids at your church are having a roller skating party and invite you to come. You would really like to go but you feel embarrassed because you don't know how to skate. What are some of your choices? What would you choose to do?

Informal Activity:

☐ ■ ☆ ★ Provide as many opportunities as possible for youth to make choices in daily life (e.g., choosing activities, making purchases, picking out clothing, and deciding what to eat). As youth gain skills, encourage their participation in more complex choice and decision making.

Goal 3: Building Friendships

For many children who have developmental differences, aspects of developing happy and healthy relationships with others need to be directly taught and practiced. We must recognize that along with learning skills, children with disabilities need increased opportunities to make friends. Therefore, some of the activities below are directed toward enhancing opportunities for developing friendships.

Activities:

1. ☐ ■ ☆ ★ For activities about friends, review the section entitled "Understanding Relationships," Goal 2, and activities 7–11.   FRIENDSHIP

2. ■ ☆ ★ As a group, create a list of attributes to look for in a good friend e.g., someone to have fun with, who you share things with, who cares what happens to you, who listens to your problems, who helps you when you are sick, and who stands up for you.

3. ■ ☆ ★ Make a similar list of ways to be a good friend.

4. ☐ ☆ ★ Complete **Friendship**, page 14 of **Me and My World Scrapbook**.

5. ☐ ■ ★ Use a relationship concentric circles mapping tool (such as the Circles program) to help students develop an understanding of how intimacy levels change   EVOLVING RE-LATIONSHIPS

☐ = Basic   ■ = Advanced   ☆ = Younger   ★ = Older

as relationships change, such as when an acquaintance becomes a close friend. (Refer to Goal 2, Activity 20 in the section entitled "Understanding Relationships" for the visual tool.)

6. ■ ☆ ★ Ask children if there is someone they would like to know better or become friends with. Make a list of things they could do to become closer to those people. Role-play one of the suggestions.

7. ■ ☆ ★ Use puppets or role-plays to demonstrate the following aspects of friendship:

> Asking someone to join a game or activity.

> Inviting a friend to come over to your house.

> Comforting a friend whose pet has died.

> Giving and receiving a gift.

> Saying "No" to a friend in a nice way.

8. ☐ ■ ☆ ★ Use the "Circle of Friends" process to develop or expand someone's friendship network. (For details about this process, refer to pages 18–21 in the section entitled "S·T·A·R·S Model.")

9. ☐ ■ ☆ ★ If you are in a school setting and the child is in a classroom only for children with special needs, plan opportunities for the child to spend time with a diverse group of peers. For example, invite another youth on a community outing, such as shopping or lunch. Support the child in joining an after school club, such as 4-H, Brownies, or Girl Scouts, and advocate for attendance at school activities, such as sporting events and dances.

ENHANCING NETWORK OF FRIENDS

10. ■ ☆ ★ Talk about the importance of personal hygiene or keeping clean in being accepted by friends. Most children are also learning about daily living skills, so activities such as combing hair, washing face and hands, and wearing clean clothes can be discussed as things we do to make ourselves attractive to others.

HYGIENE

☐ ☆ ★ Some youth may need structured instructions for hygiene activities or help keeping adequate personal hygiene. For ideas on how to use the Social Stories™ format, refer to the publication *Taking Care of Myself: A Hygiene, Puberty, and Personal Curriculum for Youth People with Autism*, by Mary Wrobel and published by Future Horizons, Inc.

☐ = Basic   ■ = Advanced   ☆ = Younger   ★ = Older

11. Etiquette and manners can also be covered. For example:

☐ ☆ ★ Saying goodbye, taking turns in conversations, and saying please and thank you.

■ ☆ ★ Role-play situations involving various social skills, such as table manners, asking politely vs. rudely, introducing someone, inviting someone, and accepting or refusing an invitation.

12. ☐ ☆ ★ Host a "gourmet" meal at home or school. Let youth practice manners at a table set with linens, flowers, and candles. Then take them to a "nice" restaurant. We can't expect them to be appropriate at fancy restaurants when they have only been to "fast food" places. Even though this can be an advanced activity, youth with all levels of skills can take part in some aspects as they are able.

13. ☐ ■ ☆ ★ Complete **I Can Use My Manners**, page 17 of **Me and My World Scrapbook**.

Informal Activities:

1. ☐ ■ ☆ ★ In natural settings, model, label, and reinforce behavior and attitudes that promote friendship and relationship building with youth.

2. ☐ ■ ☆ ★ When reading books or stories and watching TV or videos, point out examples of friendship and relationship building.

Goal 4: Engaging in More Mature Relationships

Activities:

1. ■ ★ Discuss with youth how their relationship and the ways they interact with their parents change as they get older. Note that certain ways of relating were considered ok when they were younger, but are not acceptable behaviors as they grow older. Have youth identify behaviors that are appropriate for babies and toddlers and their parents, such as:

➤ putting a child in a car seat;

➤ bathing together;

➤ changing diapers;

➤ kissing a child on the tummy;

➤ sitting on a parent's lap.

☐■★ Identify behaviors and activities that are usually appropriate for older children and their parents, such as:

➤ hugging and kissing;

➤ playing games;

➤ going places together;

➤ talking about problems;

➤ working, gardening, or performing housework together.

This activity will help lay the groundwork for understanding appropriate and inappropriate touching. Note: If you have a participant who is still using diapers or who needs assistance with personal care, acknowledge that even though the need for a parent's help may still exist, it is done differently than when the child was a baby. If appropriate, discuss with the individual feelings that he or she may have about the need for "personal" care and how it can be carried out with as much dignity as possible.

2. ☐■★ Discuss how activities with friends change as youth get older. Discuss activities that are ok for very young boys and girls to do together but that are not ok as they get older (e.g., taking baths together, running nude at the beach, and sharing bath and locker rooms).

CHANGING PEER RELATIONSHIPS

3. ■★ Review the concept of "respect" as a necessary component of a good relationship. How do people show respect? How do you know someone respects you? Role-play showing respect.

4. ■★ Introduce "romantic" relationships. Explain that teenagers and adults sometimes have friendships that develop into romantic relationships, such as between a husband and wife or two people who are dating. In a romantic relationship, people have special feelings for one another that are called "being in love."

ROMANTIC RELATIONSHIPS

☐ = Basic   ■ = Advanced   ☆ = Younger   ★ = Older

5. ■★ What is love? Discuss the different types of love a person can have. For example, loving a pet, loving nature, loving people in one's family, loving God, loving a good friend, married love (which can include family, friend, and sexual love), and sexual love.

6. ■★ What is the difference between like and love? (The depth and strength of the feelings.) Have students draw someone or something that they like and someone or something that they love. Ask them to discuss their choices.

LOVE

Some things to discuss are:

> If you are friends with someone, the relationship could remain as a friendship, and you could become really good friends.

> Sometimes when you meet or look at someone, you realize that you feel something besides friendship; you have romantic feelings. These feelings may turn into love, which is a really strong caring feeling. Love is more than physical attraction; a person's inner qualities are also important, and it takes time for love to develop. Also talk about having a strong attraction before really getting to know a person well. It might not be love, but rather infatuation.

7. ■★ Discuss what happens when you think you care about someone. One or more of the following things may happen:

> Sometimes, the other person will like you back as much as you like them, and sometimes they will like you back more or less than you like them.

> Sometimes, the other person will not be interested in a relationship with you.

> Sometimes, your feelings will change. For instance, you may not be interested anymore, or your feelings may get stronger or deeper.

8. ■★ What do we look for in a boyfriend or girlfriend? Emphasize "inner" versus "outer" or surface qualities.

9. ■★ When people who have a romantic relationship go out together, it is called dating. Note that you can also have a "date" with someone who is just a friend. Discuss the following aspects of a date:

DATING

 = Basic  = Advanced ☆ = Younger ★ = Older

> Planning the date, such as where and when it will occur, how you will get there (transportation), the phone number, the address, and the cost.

> Asking someone to go on a date, such as by phone or in person.

> Accepting or refusing a date.

> Getting ready, including hygiene and appropriate dress.

> Behavior on the date (e.g., saying good night).

Older teens with developmental disabilities are likely to need practice socializing just as they do in other areas. Role-play or help someone plan and rehearse each aspect of a date as delineated above.

More content on dating behaviors and values are included in the section entitled "Sexual Awareness."

Goal 5: Recognizing Options for Relationships into Adulthood

Today, there are many options for developing satisfying relationships in adulthood. Not all people have romantic relationships, date, and get married. It is important to give young people the opportunity to think about other possibilities and which option would feel most satisfying for them. All of us need to feel connected with other people, but satisfaction of this need may come in different forms. For some people, it might mean living with an adult foster family and having a few same-sex peers as close friends with whom to share special activities. It might mean having a special relationship with an opposite-or same-sex partner, but not necessarily one that is headed toward marriage or living together. Or it may mean marriage and parenthood.

Activities:

1. ☐ ☆ ★ Help youth list options for adult life. Help each young person think about possible options for a desirable life, recognizing that some options may be culture or family-specific. In our diverse society, options for some people may be guided by cultures, values, and norms.

   REALIZING THE POSSIBILITIES FOR THE FUTURE

2. ☐ ■ ☆ ★ Give youths the opportunity to think about options for their future, including where they might live, what type of job they may have, and possible relationships they may have. Take into consideration cultural or family influences on their choices. Think about what responsibilities these choices require and what type of support they need to accomplish their goals.

☐ = Basic   ■ = Advanced   ☆ = Younger   ★ = Older

3. ■★ With each child individually, create a story about a desirable life he or she would like to have in the future. In the story, include skills the child wants to learn and supports he or she might need to live the desired life. The story can be created by using a narrative, making a list, or selecting pictures from magazines that represent the child's dreams for the future.

These possibilities for a desirable life in the future can become a part of transition planning in the IEP process at school.

Goal 6: Building a Strong Foundation for Adult Relationships

Activities:

1. ■☆★ Show pictures from magazines of three youths who are approximately the same age as those in your group. Then, for each picture shown, ask "Who would want to be this person's friend?" Have students raise their hand, and keep a tally on the board for each picture.

   IDENTIFYING QUALITIES IN POSITIVE RELATIONSHIPS

   ➤ Ask children to pick out clues from the picture that could help them try to be the person's friend. For example, one child could have a big smile and be petting a dog. Being nice to an animal is a good thing; that person might make a good friend. Another child could be catching a baseball with a baseball mitt; you like baseball too, so that person might be a nice person to get to know.

2. ■☆★ Review the section entitled "Understanding Relationships," Goal 1, and Activity 10. Talk about the outside (physical appearance) and inside (inner qualities) things that make up a person. Remind youth that a person's inner qualities are most important when deciding whether or not to have a relationship with them and what kind of relationship it will be.

3. ■★ Ask adolescents for their ideas about the different stages or steps that two people go through on their way to developing a relationship and making a commitment to one another. It is important to realize that when discussing these stages with youth, there may be aspects of culture that need to be considered. For example, in certain cultural traditions, there are rules that women and girls must be accompanied on a date by a male family member.

   UNDERSTANDING STAGES OR "STEPS" OF RELATIONSHIPS

 = Basic    = Advanced    = Younger   = Older

> Stages include becoming friends, dating, asking yourself if this is the right person for you, courting, asking yourself if this is the right time to make a serious commitment, and marriage or partnership.

> Emphasize that it is best if these steps take some time rather than rushing into big decisions. Help adolescents realize that on television and in movies, couples seem to go through these steps or stages very quickly. In real life, it is better to take things slowly in order to get to know the person.

> Talk about each step, listing them on a large piece of paper or the blackboard. Underneath, list the specific activities that people do in each step. Review all the steps. If you are working with a youth who is in a particular stage of a relationship, discuss more specific aspects of that stage as needed. For example, under "becoming friends," you might list, with the help of participants that you do things together and talk about things you have in common. Under "asking yourself if this is the right person for you," you could list "identify the person's inner qualities."

4. ■★ Discuss marriage and other forms of committed relationships. Ask adolescents some of the reasons why they think people commit to another person. These reasons may include love, companionship, sexual attraction, respect, mutual interests, and mutual goals. Then continue the discussion with some of the wrong reasons for committing to a relationship, such as only wanting to have sex, "everyone is getting married," pressure from friends or family, and avoiding problems at home.

COMMITTED
RELATIONSHIPS

5. ■★ Individually or in a group, create a story about people who are in a committed relationship or discuss people who are in a committed relationship and who are known to the child (either personally or in the media). Help identify responsibilities of each person when in a committed relationship. These responsibilities include tasks for managing a household, such as earning money, paying bills, cooking, shopping, cleaning, doing laundry, and taking care of each other during sickness. Discuss other aspects of a committed relationship, such as mutual respect, shared goals, and expression of intimacy.

RESPONSIBILITIES
OF A COMMITTED
RELATIONSHIP

 □ = Basic   ■ = Advanced   ☆ = Younger   ★ = Older

Goal 7: Understanding the Responsibilities of Parenthood and the Pros and Cons of Having Children

Activities:

1. ■★ What must parents provide for a child in order to ensure that he or she receives adequate care? Individually or in a group, discuss the need for housing, food, clothing, health care, child care, toys, education, and discipline. What do parents need to do to provide these things for their children? Do students think that they are capable of raising children now? Or ever?

   RESPONSIBILITIES OF PARENTING

2. ■★ Role-play. Have two youths take the roles of parent and young child. The parent is trying to get the child to clean his or her room, and the child is trying to avoid the responsibility. Talk about how hard the interaction was and that parents often need to figure out ways to get their children to do things.

3. ■★ Have youth talk with a young couple who have a small child to share some of their experiences in learning about the responsibilities involved in marriage and starting a family.

4. □■☆★ Discuss other options, besides parenting, for interacting with children. Talk about roles, such as being an aunt or uncle, and work or volunteer opportunities, such as working in a day care center.

5. □■☆★ Visit a day care center so youth can observe and spend time with young children.

 = Basic    = Advanced   ☆ = Younger   = Older

Section 5:
Sexual Awareness

Goals and Activities

Along with being social, we are also sexual beings. Most children begin to discover their sexuality at an early age, when they naturally begin to touch their bodies. As they acquire language, they may ask questions, such as "Where do babies come from?" "Why don't girls have a penis?" and "Will I get breasts when I grow up?" However, sometimes children with disabilities never ask. Parents, whether they are ready for it or not, are the primary sexuality educators for their children.

How the people in a child's life respond to curiosity and provide information shapes his or her attitudes and behaviors about sex. For example, a family environment that supports a child's sensuality through appropriate touching while bathing, dressing and playing helps the child take pleasure and pride in his or her body and have an established sense of well-being. Positive early experiences provide adolescents with a good basis for responding to changes that occur during puberty. When parents share cultural and family values and beliefs youth can develop a basis for guiding their decision-making and behavior related to sexuality.

For most youth, the desire for sexual knowledge and identity continues throughout childhood and adolescence but heightens at puberty. Questions broaden and, often, the need for information expands to include issues of intimate behaviors, dating, intercourse, sexually transmitted diseases, and decision-making about sexual behavior. This is also true for many youths with disabilities, whether they actively ask questions and seek information or not.

Although early family life experiences for children with disabilities may be similar to those of children without disabilities, as adolescence approaches, life experiences may differ. Yet adolescents with disabilities are exposed to the same cultural sexual stimuli, develop secondary sex characteristics, achieve similar responses, and are expected to act responsibly, as their peers are.

Accurate information about human sexuality, including knowledge about the body and how it works, heightens self-confidence, increases self-esteem, and allays misconceptions and fears. If youth develop an understanding of the "whys" and "hows" of sexual feelings, there is a greater likelihood that self-control will be exercised, that sexuality will be expressed in acceptable and enjoyable ways, and that risks for abuse will be lessened.

Goal 1: Building a Positive Self-Image and Identity

Activities:

1. ☐ ◼ ☆ ★ Review activities in "Goal 1: Building a Positive Self Image" in the section entitled "Understanding Relationships."

    POSITIVE SELF-IMAGE

2. ☐ ☆ ★ Have each child lie on a sheet of paper large enough to trace all around the body. Help children trace and color the picture, putting clothes on their bodies. Encourage them to look at themselves in a mirror and draw what they see, filling in details such as hair and facial features. Cut the pictures out to look like people and hang them on the wall, noting the different shapes and sizes. Have each child describe something about him or herself. Children may need prompting or support to use descriptive phrases such as "curly blonde hair" and "smooth dark skin."

    BODY AWARENESS

3. ◼ ☆ ★ Ask children to (a) say something that they **like** about how they look and (b) say something that they would like to **change**, if they could.

4. ☐ ☆ ★ Compare ourselves with others and accept our differences. Use the drawings in Activity 2 to help participants identify differences in eye color, facial characteristics, hair color and texture, and body shape and size (e.g., tall or short) among the group. Note that everyone is different and that is ok. Perhaps someone in the group uses a wheelchair, has difficulty speaking, or is visually impaired; these are other examples of differences.

5. ☐ ☆ ★ Discuss ways that we take care of ourselves and keep ourselves looking good.

    ACCEPTING DIFFER-ENCES

    ➤ If appropriate for the children's level, this activity could include practicing grooming, such as hair combing, teeth brushing, and hand washing.

    ➤ Have children list things that people do every day to keep themselves healthy and looking good, such as washing and bathing, eating healthy foods, brushing teeth, getting enough sleep, brushing or combing hair, and exercising or physical activity.

    MAINTAINING PERSONAL APPEARANCE

6. ☐ ☆ ★ Complete **Looking Good and Healthy**, page 18 of **Me and My World Scrapbook**, which lists the six items above. Each day for a week, have youth mark

 ☐ = Basic   ◼ = Advanced   ☆ = Younger   ★ = Older

each activity that they completed. Younger children can use stickers, and older youth can use check marks. If a child is having difficulty completing any of the activities and this tracking system seems useful for that child, it may be beneficial to work on the activity in question (e.g., brushing teeth).

7. ■☆★ Ask the group to list other things that people do to keep themselves looking good. Include women using make-up and people wearing jewelry, going to the hair salon or barber shop (to get a permanent, style, cut, or color), wearing braces on the teeth, and getting a manicure or pedicure.

Goal 2: Identifying Gender

Note: Due to changing knowledge and attitudes about gender identification in our society, this goal may present challenges for teaching youth. Addressing these concepts may provide the opportunity to acknowledge young people who are questioning or exploring their own gender identify. In these cases, it may be helpful to connect youth with people in the community who have experience with and are sensitive to gender identify issues.

Activities:

1. ☐☆★ Help youth develop a basic understanding of gender identification. Have youth cut out pictures of males and females from magazines. Paste pictures of men and boys on one piece of paper and pictures of women and girls on another. (This activity can be done as a group or individually.) Use these pictures to identify the characteristics that students used to identify whether a person is female or male. Note whether there are similarities in dress, hairstyles, or jewelry.

UNIQUENESS OF BEING MALE OR FEMALE

2. ☐☆★ Explain to participants that before birth (at conception, when the sperm met the egg) it was determined that each person is a boy or girl.

3. ☐☆★ Have youth share whether they are male or female. Be prepared to acknowledge in a sensitive and nonjudgmental way if a youth presents him- or herself as gender variant or shares awareness about someone else who is gender variant. For example, a youth may identify as transgendered, which is an adjective describing an individual whose gender identify and assigned gender are incongruent. For instance, an individual's assigned gender may be male, but the gender identity may be female. Some individuals may also identify as having an ambiguous gender.

GENDER IDENTITY

☐ = Basic   ■ = Advanced   ☆ = Younger   ★ = Older

4. ■ ☆ ★ Help youth explore roles and behavior of men and women in today's society. Use books to show pictures of men and women engaging in non-stereotypical roles. Dispel stereotypes such as "men don't cry," "only women take care of babies," and "men are doctors, and women are teachers and nurses."

GENDER ROLES AND STEREOTYPES

Goal 3: Identifying Body Parts and Understanding Their Functions

It is important that children and youth with disabilities feel as comfortable identifying and labeling their sexual body parts as they do any other part of their bodies. Knowing about one's whole body is important for self-concept. It is also important to have words with which to communicate to others about one's sexual parts (e.g., if one of the sexual parts hurts or feels bad or if the child is injured or sexually abused).

For teaching about body parts, it is best to have pictures of children before and after puberty so participants can see the differences and identify with the picture of whichever stage their body is in. (See the Appendix for examples of such pictures.) Also, it is best to use pictures or drawings that are clear and simple and that show the internal organs as they appear in the whole body so children can visualize the location of organs. Showing only one body part as it looks separate from the body may be confusing.

A list of descriptions of body parts follows the activities for Goal 3 so you can develop your own way of describing body parts.

Activities:

1. ☐ ☆ ★ Review the location and function of nonsexual body parts with pictures, drawings, or anatomically correct dolls. Have children identify body parts in one or both of the following ways: (a) point to the body part and ask the child to name it, and (b) name the body art and ask the child to point to it. Talk about the functions of the body parts. What are arms used for? What are ears used for? What is the stomach for? Have children tell you what each body part is for either before (if they know) or after they have heard your description.

IDENTIFYING BODY PARTS AND UNDERSTANDING THEIR FUNCTIONS

> Review external body parts (those that we can see). Stick with basic body parts (e.g., arms, legs, eyes, and hair) and don't get too detailed. (Avoid parts such as phalanges and palpebral fissures.)

> Review internal body parts (those that are inside our bodies that we cannot see). Include only basic body parts, such as stomach, muscles, heart, and blood.

☐ = Basic ■ = Advanced ☆ = Younger ★ = Older

2. ☐ ☆ ★ Draw an outline of a man or a woman on a large sheet of paper leaving out all the details. Ask children if the picture is of a man or a woman and what parts they would add to the man or woman. Draw in the missing parts or have group members draw in the parts, adding as many details as they can, including genitals and body hair.

Note: For this and the following activities, be prepared to acknowledge in a sensitive and nonjudgmental way if a youth acknowledges or shares awareness about someone who may have variant sexual anatomy. (Refer to Goal 2, Activity 3 in the section entitled "Sexual Awareness.")

3. Female body parts.

☐ ☆ ★ Using the female **child** drawing in the Appendix, have children identify the sexual parts for **girls** in one of the following ways: (a) you name the part and ask children to point to it, or (b) you point to the part and ask children to name it. For the prepubertal girl, identify the breast area, the pubic area, and the vulva. Also discuss the urinary opening, anus, and vagina, which are the three openings in the girl's "bottom" or "crotch" area. These openings and the buttocks are other areas that are considered private areas. (See Goal 4 for activities related to private and public areas.)

☐ ☆ ★ Using the female **adult** drawing in the Appendix, have youth identify the sexual parts for **women** in one of the following ways: (a) you name the part and ask youth to point to it, or (b) you point to the part and ask youth to name it. At a minimum, include the breasts, vulva and pubic hair. Talk about internal parts, including the uterus, vagina, ovaries, and eggs (ova).

Also discuss the urinary opening, anus, and vagina, which are the three openings in the girl's "bottom" or "crotch" area. These openings and the buttocks are other areas that are considered private. (See Goal 4 for activities related to private and public areas.)

■ ★ In simple, understandable terms, explain the function of the female sexual parts. For example, you might say that women have two ovaries, one on each side of the lower part of the abdomen. The ovaries store the female sex cells,

IDENTIFYING SEXUAL BODY PARTS AND UNDERSTANDING THEIR FUNCTIONS

FEMALE BODY PARTS

☐ = Basic   ■ = Advanced   ☆ = Younger   ★ = Older

which are called eggs, or ova. Be careful to clarify that these eggs are not the size of the chicken eggs that we cook and eat but that they are very, very small, about the size of a pinhead. Have youth explain to you their understanding of the function of the sexual parts. See Goal 7 to include this into the discussion of sexual intercourse and conception. For youth who are capable of understanding more details, the discussion might include locating and describing the function of other female body parts, such as the clitoris and Fallopian tubes.

4. Male body parts.

☐ ☆ ★ Using the male **child** drawing in the Appendix, have children identify the sexual parts for **boys** in one of the following ways: (a) you name the part and ask children to point to it, or (b) you point to the part and ask children to name it. At a minimum, include penis, testicles, and pubic area. Also include the anus in the discussion because it is a private body part.

☐ ☆ ★ Using the male **adult** drawing in the Appendix, have youth identify the sexual parts for **men** in one of the following ways: (a) you name the part and ask children to point to it, or (b) you point to the part and ask children to name it. Include the penis, testicles, scrotum, and pubic hair. Talk about where sperm is produced. Also include the anus in the discussion because it is a private body part.

■ ★ In simple, understandable terms, explain the function of the male sexual parts. For example, sperm is the male sex cells. They are so tiny that they can't be seen without a microscope. They are produced by the testicles, and so on. Have students explain the function of the sexual parts you discussed to check their understanding. See Goal 5 in the section entitled "Sexual Awareness" to include this with the discussion of sexual intercourse and conception. For youth who are capable of understanding more details, the discussion might include specific male sexual body parts, such as the parts of the penis (e.g., the glans and shaft), scrotum, and sperm ducts.

5. ☐ ■ ☆ ★ Have children list the slang words that they have heard for each sexual part. (Explain that slang words are "made-up" words.) Explain that some people get upset when they hear those words or they don't understand what the term

> MALE BODY PARTS

> SLANG WORDS

means. It is best to remember the "real" word for the sexual part, which may also be called the dictionary word.

6.  Discuss that everyone's body looks different, including their sexual parts. Just as hair and eye color differ, so do body height and weight and the size and shape of sexual body parts. For example, talk about the fact that some women have small breasts and some women have large breasts, while some men have a small penis and some men have a large penis. Even though we are all different, we are still "ok."

BODY PARTS

Anus: An opening that acts as a passageway for the elimination of solid waste in the body.

Bladder: The hollow organ inside the body of both men and women that holds urine.

Breasts: Both men and women have breasts. However, a woman's breasts grow larger than a man's during puberty and can produce milk after childbirth. Breasts are also a source of sexual pleasure in most women and some men.

Cervix: The narrow, lower end of the uterus. It has a small opening into the vagina called the cervical opening that lets the menstrual fluid, or "period" flow out. It also lets a man's sperm travel into the uterus and Fallopian tubes. During childbirth, the cervical opening can stretch wide enough to let a baby pass through; after childbirth, it shrinks back down to its normal size.

Clitoris: A small sensitive sex organ in a woman. It is about the size of a pea and is located in the soft folds of the skin that meet just above the vagina and urethra. It has many nerve endings and is very sensitive. Pleasurable feelings result when the clitoris is touched during lovemaking, sexual intercourse, or masturbation. Stimulating the clitoris is the main way that most women reach a climax.

Egg cell: A tiny cell; it is the woman's reproductive cell. It is also called an ovum or ova (plural). It comes out of one of a woman's ovaries each month and travels down the Fallopian tube to the uterus. These eggs are very small, not the size of the chicken eggs that we cook and eat, and can only be seen with a microscope. If a man's sperm joins an egg cell, the egg and sperm together will grow into a baby.

Genitals: The name for the sex organs or sex parts that are on the outside of a man or woman. In a man, these are the penis, testicles, and scrotum. In a woman, they include the vulva, vagina, and clitoris. In rare circumstances, individuals may have genital anomalies.

Ovaries: Two very small organs, or sacks, inside a woman's body that hold the tiny egg cells, or ova. Beginning in puberty, each month one egg leaves one ovary and travels down the Fallopian tube and into the uterus. The ovaries make estrogen and progesterone, the female hormones that regulate the menstrual cycle.

Penis: The man's sex organ that hangs between his legs. When a man gets sexually excited, the penis becomes hard. During sexual intercourse, it is used to go inside a woman's vagina. The penis is also used by men to urinate.

Pubic area: The place between the legs in both women and men where the external genital organs are located. It's covered with pubic hair, which starts to grow at puberty.

Scrotum: The wrinkled sack of skin that hangs behind a man's penis. The scrotum holds the two testicles, which make sperm.

Semen: The thick white liquid that comes out of a man's penis when he has a climax, or orgasm. Sperm is in the semen.

Sex organs: Another name for sexual body parts.

Sperm: Tiny male reproductive cells that are made in a man's testicles. When a man is sexually excited, his penis gets hard. He can have an orgasm, and the semen, which contains sperm cells, is released from the opening in the penis, called ejaculation. If a man ejaculates inside a woman's vagina, the sperm cells swim up through her uterus and into the Fallopian tubes. If a sperm cell finds, and enters, a woman's egg cell in her tubes, fertilization occurs. Boys start making sperm cells sometime during adolescence.

Testicles: Two glands located inside the scrotum. These glands make sperm cells and a male hormone called testosterone. The testicles start making sperm cells sometime during adolescence and continue until old age.

Urethra: The tube that carries urine from the bladder to the outside of the body. Men urinate from the penis. Women urinate from the opening between the vagina and clitoris.

Uterus: The uterus is a pear-shaped organ located at the end of the vagina inside a woman's abdomen. The lining of the uterus builds up each month in preparation for an egg. If the egg cell isn't fertilized, the lining is shed about once a month, a process called menstruation. When a woman is pregnant, the uterus stretches to hold the developing fetus and shrinks down after the baby is born.

Vagina: A passage in a woman that leads from the external sex organs (between her legs) to the uterus. During intercourse, the man puts his penis in the vagina. The menstrual blood flows down the vagina and out of the woman's body; this is where a tampon fits during a period. The vagina also stretches during childbirth to allow the baby to pass through.

Vulva: The soft folds of skin around a woman's vagina.

Goal 4: Understanding Public and Private Behavior

Activities:

1. ☐ ☆ ★ Review the concepts of "privacy" and "private."

   PRIVATE AND PRIVACY

   ➤ We all have the right to be alone (privacy) at times.

   ➤ Your body belongs to you.

   ➤ Your body has private parts.

   ➤ Some activities are private and need to be done in private places, usually when no one else is around.

   ➤ Social media is not a private place.

   ➤ You should not touch another person unless he or she wants to be touched.

   ➤ In most cases, no one should touch you unless you want to be touched.

2. ☐ ☆ ★ Help youth identify their private places, such as at home (e.g., bedroom and bathroom) and at school (e.g., a cubby, locker, desk, or bathroom). Complete **My Private Spaces** and **My Private Things**, page 13 of **Me and My World Scrapbook**. Also talk about the importance of each person respecting the privacy of others. Youth may want to make or have a "PRIVATE" sign to use.

   PRIVATE PLACES

3. ☐ ☆ ★ Discuss which parts of the body are considered private. Talk about sexual and other related parts, including genital areas, breasts, and buttocks. Using the drawings in the Appendix (male and female adult or child, depending on the needs of the youth), have youth identify the **private** parts of the body. Youth can then show their understanding of the concept by drawing or pasting on pictures of underwear or a bathing suit to cover the private parts. Anatomically correct dolls are also great for demonstrating this concept. Discuss that there are certain times when it is ok for certain people, such as a parent, nurse, physician, or other caregiver, to touch your private parts, such as when you are sick or hurt.

   PRIVATE BODY PARTS

4. ☐ ☆ ★ Discuss "private" activities and behavior: that is, things we do in private places when other people are not around. Help children think about activities that are done in private places. Include bathing, taking a shower, using the toilet, undressing

   PRIVATE ACTIVITIES

and dressing, touching your own sexual parts for pleasure. (Depending on the age of youth, decide whether to use the term masturbation.) The use of pictures might be useful to demonstrate the abstract concept of "private." For older youth who may be dating, you might include sexual behaviors such as kissing, "necking," and "petting."

Note: This is a good time to stress the importance of not posting or sharing pictures or anyone's private parts on social media.

5. ☐ ☆ ★ Introduce the concept of "public." Explain that public is associated with other people.

6. ☐ ☆ ★ Help youth identify public places. Emphasize that "public" usually means that other people are around, such as at home (e.g., the kitchen, living room, and yard), at school (e.g., the classroom and playground), and in the community (e.g., the store and bus stop). Combine with Activity 2.

PUBLIC

7. ☐ ■ ☆ ★ Discuss which parts of the body are considered public. This may vary according to cultural beliefs or family background. Illustrate this concept by using age-appropriate drawings of people (see the Appendix for examples) to point out the public parts—those that it is ok for other people to see. Remind youth that even if a body part is a public part, "you don't have to be touched there if you don't want to." Anatomically correct dolls are also useful for demonstrating this concept. Combine this discussion with Activity 3.

PUBLIC PLACES

PUBLIC BODY PARTS

8. ☐ ☆ ★ Discuss public activities or behavior, including those things that are ok to do in front of other people. Combine this discussion with Activity 4. Acknowledge possible cultural differences.

9. Meet individual needs of youth regarding private and public.

☐ ■ ☆ ★ You may need to discuss the fact that some youth need help with bathing and toileting, which might require the caregiver to touch private parts in order to assist with an activity that is considered private and occurs in a private place. Discuss this individually with youth as needed.

PUBLIC ACTIVITIES

☐ ☆ ★ For some youth to be accepted and learn acceptable social behavior, it may be necessary to give individualized instruction with specific rules about private and public behavior and places. For example, it may be ok to touch themselves,

DIFFER-ENTIATING PRIVATE & PUBLIC

☐ = Basic   ■ = Advanced   ☆ = Younger   ★ = Older

or masturbate, in the shower or bathroom at home (which are private places), but it is not ok to touch themselves or masturbate in the bathroom or shower while at school (which are more like public places).

☐ ☆ ★ As the caregiver, think about how you respond to a child if he or she engages in a private activity (e.g., masturbation) in a non-private or public place. It is usually best to interrupt the behavior and give information about if, when, and where the behavior is ok. Then redirect the child to another activity. Try to teach rather than scold.

10. ■ ☆ ★ Help youth differentiate among private and public places and activities. Give children two 3" × 5" cards, one of which says "private" and the other of which says "public." Using a set of cards that list activities and places, hold up each card separately and have youth either point to or hold up one of their cards. Body parts can also be added to the cards.

Goal 5: Differentiating Between Inappropriate and Appropriate Touching

Activities:

1. ■ ☆ ★ Review private and public body parts by using the drawings of the boy, girl, man, and woman in the Appendix or anatomically correct dolls. Which parts can be shown in public? Which parts are covered in public? Use cut-outs of clothing, such as underwear, bathing suits, and winter clothing, to cover the drawings and help students understand private and public.

   PRIVATE AND PUBLIC BODY PARTS

   Recognize cultural differences in private and public body parts. For example, some Muslim women cover their heads in public.

2. ■ ☆ ★ Talk about private and public behavior and activities. See Goal 4, Activities 4 and 8.

   PRIVATE AND PUBLIC BEHAVIOR

3. ■ ☆ ★ Talk about people who may and may not be allowed to touch your private parts. Sometimes doctors, nurses, personal caregivers, moms, or dads need to check private parts if you are sick or hurt. Otherwise, it is not ok for anyone to touch your private parts.

☐ = Basic   ■ = Advanced   ☆ = Younger   ★ = Older

4. ☐ ☆ ★ Help children identify the different types of touches.

TYPES OF "TOUCHES"

> "Good" touches: a nurturing touch that feels like something is being given or shared, such as a hug, holding hands with your mother, having your sister brush your hair, and having your back rubbed. Think about how nice these things feel.

> "Bad" touches: a touch that is painful or feels like something is being taken away, such as when someone kicks or bites you, a mosquito bite, and bruising your knee when you fall down. Think about how bad or "yucky" these things feel. This could also be when someone touches you in a private place (as in sexual abuse) or in a way that feels bad or that you don't want.

> "Confusing" touches: a touch that cannot be clearly labeled as good or bad. Any touch may be confusing when (a) the meaning of the touch is unclear, (b) the person being touched is not accustomed to the touch or doesn't want to be touched, or (c) the touching becomes sexual and the person being touched is confused about it. For example, sometimes things that are listed as good touches don't feel good, like being hugged by a relative when you don't want to be hugged. Another example is when someone you like and, who is usually nice to you, touches you in a way that feels uncomfortable, tickling you for too long or touching you in a private place.

5. ■ ☆ ★ Present different situations to help youth figure out inappropriate touching by combining aspects of public and private and socially appropriate behavior. For example, "Is it ok to touch your brother's penis?" "Is it ok to touch your own penis or vagina when you are in a public place?"

In the section entitled "Assertiveness," there are activities for learning how to avoid or respond to unwanted touches.

Goal 6: Understanding the Emotional and Physical Changes of Puberty

The discussion of puberty should be timed in youths' lives so that the information makes sense and is most functional for them. Often, a discussion of body changes and menstruation just before the age of puberty is the best time. Be sure to consider parental and community values and attitudes before proceeding with this information. Some parents may have strong feelings about whether they want their child to participate in the discussion and what type of information their child should receive. The **Letter to Parent or Guardian**, which describes the Sexuality Education Program, in the Appendix, is one way to inform parents and seek their consent about your instruction.

☐ = Basic   ■ = Advanced   ☆ = Younger   ★ = Older

Most of the discussion and teaching can be done with boys and girls together, although some may be more comfortable having the boys and girls separated.

Activities:

1. ☐ ■ ☆ ★ Draw a long line on a large piece of paper (about four to five feet long) taped to the wall. Together with children, count to 21 while writing the numbers on the line, leaving space after 21 for older adults. You might explain that each number is another birthday in our lives and that each year we grow a little more and our appearance changes. Help youth cut pictures from magazines that illustrate people of all ages, from infancy to adulthood. Ask children to bring in pictures of themselves at various ages. Then, as a group, decide where along the number line to put the pictures. Have children identify which pictures look like babies, children, teenagers, and grown-ups. How can they tell? Help them identify height, size, facial hair, breasts, etc. Help children name each group: babies, children, teenagers, and adults.

   UNDERSTANDING DEVELOPMENTAL STAGES

2. ☐ ☆ ★ Explain puberty using simple terms and understandable ideas. For example, you might include that at a certain point in your life, your body will know that it's time to begin changing to become a grown-up. This time is called puberty, and your body begins to change to look more like a grown-up (e.g., moms and dads). Changes take place both inside and outside the body, some of which are obvious, and others of which we cannot see. Have youth tell you about puberty to check their understanding.

   UNDERSTANDING PUBERTY

3. ☐ ☆ ★ Identify body changes that occur during puberty. Help youth identify specific characteristics that make grown-ups **look** different from children: They are taller, have body hair, have breasts, and have big muscles. Use pictures of children and adults to demonstrate these differences. Use the developmental chart with pictures in Goal 4, Activity 1 in the section entitled "Sexual Awareness" to help identify these differences.

   BODY CHANGES DURING PUBERTY

   In girls, the following changes appear in puberty: breasts start to enlarge, pubic hair appears, hair appears under the arms, height increases, and menstruation begins.

☐ = Basic   ■ = Advanced   ☆ = Younger   ★ = Older

In boys, the following changes appear in puberty: testes and penis get bigger, pubic hair appears, voice changes, ejaculation becomes possible (this may be an advanced concept), height increases, hair appears under arms, and facial hair appears.

Be sensitive to the possibility that body changes in some children may occur outside of typical development.

4. ☐ ■ ★ If adolescents are near or in the midst of puberty, and it feels comfortable, have them identify changes they have noticed in their own bodies. Be sensitive about this; for some youth, this activity may be too uncomfortable.

5. ■ ★ Talk about other more subtle changes, including emotions, such as feeling awkward, moody, or embarrassed; being tired or energetic; having body odor or sweating; and gaining or losing weight.

6. ■ ★ Discuss some of the body changes that occur during puberty in greater detail.

   ➤ Underarms may sweat more. Underarm hair will grow.

   ➤ Girls may start shaving their underarm area and legs.

   ➤ Boys begin to grow facial hair and begin shaving.

   ➤ Pubic hair grows for both boys and girls. It may be a different color than the hair on the head.

   ➤ Both boys and girls need to shower or bathe more often to keep odors away. Both boys and girls use deodorant.

   ➤ Breasts grow larger, and girls begin to wear a bra. Some may experience some breast discomfort. Breast self-examinations begin.

7. ☐ ■ ★ Explain that during puberty, girls experience sexual changes. Most girls experience an increase in sexual feelings in addition to their body changes. Having sexy dreams and fantasies and becoming sexually excited is a normal part of growing up. In the discussion, emphasize that it is not necessary to act on these feelings or arousal just because the girl has become aware of them.

CHANGES IN FEMALES

For girls, an important aspect of puberty is that they begin **menstruation**, or their "**period**." Use simple and understandable words. Think about what level of information is needed for each girl. There is a wide spectrum of needs. Not everything may be appropriate or needed for each person. Consider whether the girl needs

MENSTRUATION

just enough information so she won't become frightened when her period starts, whether more information would be too abstract and confusing for her, or whether she needs a lot of information because she has higher capabilities and can understand that a girl can become pregnant if she is menstruating.

> You can say that menstruation only happens to girls. It begins during puberty, when a girl's body is developing and she starts to become a woman. It is a natural process, and there is nothing to be afraid of. Menstruation is also called a period. It happens monthly until women are in their 40's or 50's. Remind girls about the vagina, which is the middle opening in their "bottom" area. Use pictures and an anatomically correct doll to show as explicitly as possible where menstrual blood comes from. Have girls tell you about menstruation to check their understanding. Include slang words for menstruation, as well as the "dictionary" word.

> Boys will also benefit from basic information about menstruation if it helps them better understand the female body, what girls go through, and any misinformation. Boys will be curious about feminine hygiene products (e.g., menstrual pads and tampons), which are very visible in our culture. Boys should be given a brief explanation and an opportunity to see these products. However, some of the more explicit discussion and use of feminine hygiene products may be best done with only girls.

8. ■★ Point out that when a girl is mature enough to menstruate, her body has gone through changes that make it possible for her to become pregnant. See Goal 7 for activities regarding intercourse and pregnancy. Ask female adolescents whether they think that because their bodies can produce eggs like a woman if they are old enough and capable enough to be a mother (and a wife). Ask youth to tell you their understanding of this.

9. □■★ With girls, demonstrate the use of feminine hygiene products. Girls will benefit from the opportunity to practice handling the hygiene products and will probably feel more comfortable doing this without boys present. It is useful to explain that the blood is not like that from a cut on the outside of the body, which is red, quite liquid, and clots. Instead, menstrual blood usually starts out slowly and is brownish in color. It may get redder, but it is usually thicker and doesn't flow out of the body the same way. You can illustrate this by using hair gel and food coloring mixed together on a menstrual pad to explicitly show the consistency of menstrual blood. Have girls practice with a sanitary

FEMININE HYGIENE PRODUCTS

 = Basic   = Advanced   ☆ = Younger   = Older

pad with adhesive on a pair of clean panties. Have them give a repeat demonstration to check their skills. Teach girls the proper way to wrap and dispose of used sanitary napkins. Tampon use can also be taught, although it is best done on a one-to-one basis.

10. ☐ ■ ★ Identify specific adults who could help girls both at home and at school at the start of or during their period. Such adults might include their parents, sisters, physical education teacher, school nurse, classroom teacher or aide, and the school secretary. Help girls locate where to keep their feminine hygiene supplies at home, at school, and when they go out in the community.

11. ■ ★ Discuss other concerns about menstruation, including cramps, recording menstrual cycles, and premenstrual syndrome (PMS). Explain that there is no need to restrict activity during menstruation.

12. ☐ ■ ★ Explain that boys experience sexual changes during puberty. Most boys experience an increase in sexual feelings, causing more frequent erections of their penis, which is normal. Having sexy dreams and fantasies and becoming sexually excited is a normal part of growing up. Emphasize, though, that it is not necessary to act on sexual feelings just because youth become aware of these feelings.

> CHANGES IN BOYS

Explain an **erection** using simple and understandable terms. Figure out how much detail to use based on the understanding capabilities of the boys. Show pictures of men to compare the penis in its flaccid and erect states. Discuss the slang words for erection, as well as the word erection.

> ERECTION

> In a basic discussion, you might say that an erection is when the penis gets stiff and hard when a boy or man is sexually excited. It can happen often when a boy is going through puberty and sometimes results from seeing a sexually attractive person or from physical stimulation from clothing or touching. It happens less often as boys mature. Remind adolescents that if an erection happens when they are in a public place, it is not ok to touch their penis. Sometimes ejaculation occurs with an erection. See Activity 14 for an explanation of ejaculation.

> Girls will also benefit from basic information about male body functions. It will help them better understand the male body, what boys are going through, and any misinformation. If presenting information in a group setting, the decision to share this information with a co-ed group or with boys and girls separately depends on the comfort level of the adult facilitator and the individual boys and girls.

 ☐ = Basic   ■ = Advanced   ☆ = Younger   ★ = Older

13. ■★ Discuss erection in more detail, linking it with intercourse if the boys have the capability to understand.

 ➤ You might say that men and boys are built the way they are and have erections because it is part of the process of creating babies. A man's penis is designed to be able to fit inside a woman's vagina, and it needs to be erect to do that. Have the boys tell you about erection to check their understanding.

 ➤ Identify the slang words for erection.

14. ■★ Explain **ejaculation**. Use simple, understandable terms. You might say that when older boys and men are sexually excited, the penis has an erection. If the penis is stimulated enough, the adolescent or man will have an orgasm, which is a very strong and good feeling in the area around the penis. At the time of the orgasm, a thick white fluid called semen, which carries sperm, quickly comes out (about a tablespoonful) from the end of the penis. Have boys tell you about ejaculation to check their understanding.

> EJACULATION

 ➤ Often during puberty, boys experience "wet dreams," which occur when they ejaculate during their sleep. Not all boys have wet dreams during puberty, but many do. Emphasize that wet dreams are normal, that boys can't do anything to stop themselves from having them, and that once they are through puberty, the wet dreams will probably stop.

 ➤ Identify the slang words for ejaculation.

15. ■★ Have youth discuss what privileges they might have as they get older, such as earning money, having more privacy, being more independent, being able to date, choosing their own clothes in the store, and staying up later. Keep in mind variations among cultures.

> PRIVILEGES WHEN GROWING UP

Goal 7: Understanding Sexual Feelings and Behaviors

Activities:

1. ■★ Review romantic relationships. See Goal 4 in the section entitled "Social Interaction."

2. ■★ It is important for youth to understand what behaviors are considered sexual,

> SEXUAL EXPRESSION

□ = Basic   ■ = Advanced   ☆ = Younger   ★ = Older

as well as the range of sexual behaviors that can be associated with a romantic relationship. It is also important to consider cultural and family values along with social rules that are related to sexual expression. (See Goal 8.) List behaviors that two people in a romantic relationship might do to express their affection for one another, including giving compliments and gifts, holding hands, hugging, kissing, "necking," "petting," and having sexual intercourse. Clarify what these terms mean. For example, "necking," or "making out," means having a prolonged kissing session. Help youth understand which behaviors are ok in a romantic relationship and are not ok in other relationships.

3. ■★ Discuss sexual orientation. Some people have or want a sexual partner of the opposite sex to care about and have sex with; this sexual orientation is called heterosexual. Other people have or want a sexual partner of the same sex to care about and have sex with; this sexual orientation is called homosexual. Use the correct terminology: A female homosexual is also called a lesbian, and a male homosexual is also called gay. For more discussion activities, see Goal 9: Examining Societal Norms and Values Regarding Sexuality in the section entitled "Sexual Awareness."

SEXUAL ORIENTATION

4. □■☆★ Explain **masturbation.** You might say that masturbation is when boys or girls touch their own sexual parts (i.e., private parts or genitals) by stroking or rubbing them, which feels very nice. Use an illustration. Emphasize that masturbation is done in a private place, and identify possible places with adolescents. See Goal 4, Activity 4 in the section entitled "Sexual Awareness" to combine this discussion with that about private and public behavior. See Goal 9, Activity 1 in the section entitled "Sexual Awareness" to combine this discussion with values about sexual behavior.

MASTURBATION

5. ■★ Explain **orgasm.** Orgasm happens in women and men. You might say that when a person (male or female) is sexually excited, sometimes he or she experiences a build-up of sexual, or erotic, tension. The heart might beat faster and stronger, breathing may be more rapid, and muscles may tense. This muscle tension increases to a certain level until there is a release, which is often somewhat sudden. After the release, there is usually a feeling of well-being, relaxation, or relief. In women, orgasm usually involves the clitoris and surrounding area. In men, orgasm involves the penis, scrotum, and surrounding pelvic area. It can happen as a result of masturbation or intercourse. In men, ejaculation is not the same

ORGASM

 = Basic    = Advanced   ☆ = Younger   ★ = Older

as orgasm, but they usually happen together. See Goal 6, Activities 12 and 14, for more discussion on ejaculation.

6. ■★ Explain **intercourse**. First, review male and female sexual body parts, including the penis and vagina, then review erection. Your explanation must be simple and understandable. You might say that when a grown-up man and a grown-up woman love each other very much in a sexual way, they may want to have intercourse. While they are in a private place, both the man and woman usually get sexually excited by kissing, hugging, and touching each other on their bodies, including their private parts. When a man gets sexually excited, his penis will become erect, and when a woman gets excited, her vagina may become moist from secretions. Intercourse is when the man puts his erect penis inside the woman's vagina. Moving back and forth can feel very good for both the man and the woman and usually causes the man to ejaculate sperm and the woman to have an orgasm. This is the way that a woman can become pregnant.

INTERCOURSE

➤ This discussion might be tied into the discussion on prevention of pregnancy or contraception.

➤ Emphasize the benefits of having a monogamous relationship.

7. ■★ Explain the word **virgin**. You might say that "virgin" is a word to describe a woman or a man who has never had sexual intercourse.

VIRGIN

Reinforce that there is nothing wrong with being a virgin. It is a healthy choice and is relatively typical, especially for adolescents. Youth should not have sexual intercourse because of peer pressure.

Goal 8: Understanding Reproduction

Activities:

1. ■★ Explain fertilization. Review internal and external sexual body parts, which are discussed in Goal 3 in the section entitled "Sexual Awareness," and intercourse, which is discussed in Goal 7, Activity 6, in the section entitled "Sexual

FERTILIZATION

 = Basic    = Advanced    = Younger   = Older

Awareness." In the discussion, you might say that if it is the time of the month when a woman's ovary has produced an egg (or an ovum), which usually occurs between periods, the act of intercourse could result in fertilization and a pregnancy. Fertilization and pregnancy occur when the egg meets with the sperm, is fertilized, and then attaches to the uterine wall. In your discussion, be clear about the size of the egg: It is very tiny, not like chicken eggs. Do not use terminology like "planting a seed," as some books suggest. People with cognitive disabilities usually think very concretely, and youth could take this to mean that if they want to have a baby, they should plant a seed, like an apple or watermelon seed, in their vagina rather than understanding that pregnancy results from sexual intercourse. Have youth explain fertilization to check their understanding.

2. ■★ Discuss pregnancy. In most cases, pregnancy happens after a man and a woman have intercourse and fertilization occurs. The egg in the woman meets with the sperm from the man after intercourse and starts growing in the woman's uterus. Pregnancy normally lasts nine months. After about four months, the mother's abdomen begins to get noticeably larger as the baby grows inside the uterus. Clarify that the baby does not grow in the stomach, where the food goes, but rather in the uterus. Have students tell you about pregnancy by using pictures or anatomically correct dolls to check their understanding.

PREGNANCY

➤ Be prepared to acknowledge that youth may share knowledge or experiences about other means of fertilization and pregnancy.

➤ You might want to discuss the concept of twins or multiple births.

➤ Other areas for discussion, especially for older students who have the capability to understand, might include how a woman knows she is pregnant. Talk about having intercourse, missing a period, noticing some physical changes, and going to the doctor for a pregnancy test.

3. ■★ Explain the labor and birthing process to help students understand how the baby gets out of the mother's body. How does the baby get out? Birth of a baby usually happens in the hospital, where doctors and nurses can help. Include both types of births: vaginal delivery and Cesarean section. Pictures or anatomic models that show the whole woman's body during delivery are helpful. (Sometimes,

LABOR AND DELIVERY

 = Basic    = Advanced    = Younger   = Older

science or home economics classrooms have these materials.) Explain that labor and birth are a lot of work and that many women say that it is painful but worth it.

> Explain the umbilical cord and the umbilicus, or belly button. The baby and mother are connected inside by the umbilical cord of the baby and the inside of the mother's uterus (the placenta) so that the baby gets enough nourishment and oxygen. Once the baby is outside the mother's body, this cord, or connection, isn't needed anymore and is cut off. The resulting belly button is where this cord was located.

> Sometimes a film or video of the birthing process is useful for those youth who are capable of understanding. However, think carefully about whether this is helpful for youth to see and for whom. Always be sure to preview the film or video before showing. Also, be certain to prepare youth for what they will see.

4. ■★ Discuss preventing pregnancy. Include (a) abstaining from, or not having, intercourse, and (b) contraceptive methods as possible ways to prevent pregnancy (See #5 through #9 below for specific information.)

PREVENTION OF PREGNANCY

With adolescents, you can share the message that parents and teachers hope that teenagers won't get sexually involved until they are mature enough to handle it but that if the decision is made to have intercourse, it is recommended that birth control is used.

Planned Parenthood is an excellent resource for obtaining birth control.

5. ■★ Abstaining from, or not having intercourse. Adolescents need to know that it is ok to have sexual feelings but that sexual intercourse doesn't have to be the only way to express those feelings. In your discussion, identify ways to avoid situations in which intercourse can easily happen. For example, you could choose social activities in a group instead of with only your intimate partner, recognizing that it may be hard to stop yourself if you and your partner are in a private place and get sexually excited. Remind adolescents that they can make their own decisions and don't have to worry about pleasing their boyfriend or girlfriend or giving in to peer pressure.

NOT HAVING INTERCOURSE

 = Basic  = Advanced  = Younger = Older

In your discussion, include the strong health and developmental reasons for adolescents to abstain from having intercourse. Some of these reasons include:

➤ The high risk for contracting sexually transmitted diseases.

➤ The dangers of exploitation for both young women and men.

➤ The risk for pregnancy.

Girls may emotionally mature later than boys, even though they physically mature earlier. Early first sexual experiences are often very unsatisfactory.

6. ■★ Discuss contraception, or birth control. For youth to best understand, a discussion of contraception should follow a review of intercourse and the process of fertilization. See Goal 7, Activity 6, and Goal 8, Activity 1, in the section entitled "Sexual Awareness." Clarify for students that if they have intercourse and do not use contraception, it is possible that the girl will become pregnant.

You might explain that when a man and a woman are very much in love and want to show their love through intercourse but do not want to have a baby, they can prevent pregnancy by using **birth control** or **contraception**, which stops the sperm and egg from coming together to produce a baby.

Not all adolescents with developmental disabilities need to have detailed information about birth control. If a youth can understand intercourse, then he or she likely can understand the concept of birth control. The most essential information to provide about birth control is its general purpose, why it is used, when to use it, and who adolescents can talk to get help with birth control. Presenting many specific types of birth control measures at one time may be confusing for youths, especially if they have a cognitive disability. Instead, if youth need more specific information about birth control, they would best benefit from a one-to-one conversation with a helping adult. Direct them to the best type of birth control for their abilities and situation.

7. ■★ Tell youth that there are many different types of birth control and that there are people they can talk to about it. Depending on the setting, help them identify who they can talk to, such as a specific teacher, school nurse, guidance counselor, or family planning clinic in the community. It is still likely that youth with disabilities will need individualized support in obtaining birth control.

 = Basic    = Advanced    = Younger   = Older

Acknowledge that there may be religious, family, or cultural beliefs related to the use of birth control.

8. ■★ Provide specific instructions for the use of birth control methods as indicated. For example, condoms are used to prevent pregnancy and transmission of autoimmune deficiency syndrome (AIDS) and other sexually transmitted diseases. Condoms are readily available in stores, and many adolescents have heard of them.

Students with cognitive disabilities will need explicit information about condom use: that is, exactly when and how to use one. Do not make anyone uncomfortable by demonstrating use of a condom on a human, but **do** demonstrate its use on a life-sized model of a penis. Be sure to explain the specifics of condom use. You might say that once the penis is erect, and **before** intercourse, you put the condom on by placing it on the tip of the penis and gently unrolling it down toward the body. Other essential information might include that latex condoms are the safest kind; that condoms should be kept in their wrappers for no longer than six months to avoid breakage or tearing; and that buying condoms with nonoxynyl-9, a jelly-like substance that acts as a spermicide helps prevent pregnancy.

9. ■★ Explain sterilization. Sterilization includes methods of birth control that are permanent and is suitable only for those men and women who have decided that they never want to cause conception or become pregnant. (There are laws about who can be sterilized. See the Appendix for references that provide further information.)

STERILIZATION

10. ■★ Explain abortion. You can say that abortion is a surgical procedure done by a licensed physician (i.e., a medical doctor) to end a pregnancy before the time when the baby would be grown enough to be born, usually sometime within one through four months. Emphasize that an abortion is a serious procedure to remove the fetus and the placenta and that it is performed by a doctor in a medical clinic or hospital. You must never attempt to perform an abortion yourself. Abortion should not be substituted for the use of other birth control measures. People have differing views on whether it is ethical or moral, and the legal availability of abortion varies greatly among states in the U.S.

ABORTION

Goal 9: Examining Societal Norms and Values Regarding Mature Sexual Behavior

Note: For this section, it is important to acknowledge possible variations among cultural and family beliefs that may affect acceptable sexual behavior.

☐ = Basic   ■ = Advanced   ☆ = Younger   ★ = Older

Activities:

1. ■★ In a group or individual discussion, create a list of different sexual activities, such as hugging, kissing, sexual touching with a partner, masturbation, and sexual intercourse. Discuss each activity separately. Present the concept of values and social rules as things that tell us how to act in an acceptable way. For example, "What rules do your parents tell you?" "What rules are there in school?" List values or social rules for each of the sexual activities (i.e., when the behaviors are ok and when they are not).

   For example, discuss:

   How well should you know someone before you touch each other in a sexual way?

   ➤ When is it ok to have sexual intercourse? You might start the discussion with, "Some people have strong feelings about sexual intercourse and that it is only ok if the man and woman are married. Other people have different values or ideas and feel that if two people care about each other very much and want to express their love with sexual intercourse, it is ok, even if they are not married. What do you think?"

   ➤ Masturbation is another value-laden behavior. Your discussion may include the following points: Is it ok to masturbate? When and where might it be ok? People have different ideas about masturbation: Some people think that it is terrible and should never be done, and other people think that it is normal and healthy and ok in a private place.

   ➤ Homosexuality. Our society is moving towards greater acceptance and granting rights, including marriage, to individuals who identify as homosexual. However, some people do not accept homosexuality as a sexual orientation. There are slang terms that are rude to use, such as "fag," "dyke," and "homo"; remind youth that these words are hurtful and that it is best not to use them.

2. ■★ Present the concept of mutual consent in sexual behavior. Mutual consent means that both people agree that the sexual behavior is ok, whether it is touching, hugging, kissing, or intercourse. If either of the people does not agree to the behavior, it is never ok to do these behaviors. Talk about sexual assault, including the spectrum of unwanted sexual touching to rape. See the section entitled "Assertiveness" for specifics on personal safety.

INFLUENCE OF SOCIAL RULES AND PERSONAL VALUES ON SEXUAL BEHAVIOR

MUTUAL CONSENT

 = Basic    = Advanced    = Younger   = Older

3. ■★ Make decisions about sexual situations. This discussion makes the most sense when youth are dating or thinking about a relationship.

PERSONAL DECISION-MAKING

Discuss some important things to think about when making decisions about showing sexual feelings. During adolescence, abstinence, or not having sexual intercourse, is preferred. However, without information and support, some adolescents may have difficulty abstaining from sexual intercourse. Youth will need help understanding the concept of abstinence and figuring out ways to manage their feelings and peer pressure. This section may be useful in helping youth who are in serious relationships consider their behavior.

> Do you feel like you're ready and that you can be responsible for your actions, which affect both you and the other person?

> Be sure that the other person feels the same way you do. Never force anyone to do **anything**.

> If you can, discuss these issues with your family so you know their feelings and values. If that is difficult, find another trustworthy adult you can talk with. Who could that adult be?

> Think about sexual behavior ahead of time.

How does a person know that he or she is ready for a sexual relationship? To be ready to engage in sexual behavior, it is best if a person can:

> Understand that the enjoyment of this aspect of sexuality involves the ability to make thoughtful decisions.

> Comfortably discuss, either verbally or through augmentative communication, precautions against unintended pregnancy and sexually transmitted diseases with his or her partner and share responsibility for taking them.

> Be sure that he or she is not exploiting another person or being exploited themselves.

> Be willing to make the emotional commitment and take on the obligation of a healthy adult sexual relationship.

4. ■★ Sometimes it is easier for adolescents to use a story about someone else to discuss decision-making. Use pictures in books or magazines, and develop a story with which adolescents can relate.

 □ = Basic   ■ = Advanced   ☆ = Younger   ★ = Older

For example, this story makes the point that there are other ways to express feelings and be with your intimate sexual partner than just having sex. "In this picture, suppose that Joe and Sharon care about each other very much and have very strong emotional feelings for each other. They have both decided that they are not ready for sexual intercourse, but they want to share their sexual feelings. What are some other ways they can show their affection?" (See Goal 7, Activities 1–3, in the section entitled "Sexual Awareness," to review sexual behaviors in romantic relationships.) "How can they figure out what they will do?" Answers include talking to each other and talking to a trusted adult to help give suggestions.

Present other brief situations and ask students for their opinions about what they would do. List two to three alternatives for each situation and then discuss what the consequences of that decision might be. Influence of Social Rules and Personal Values on Sexual Behavior

Goal 10: Learning about Sexually Transmitted Diseases

Activities:

1. ■★ To help youth grasp the concept of sexually transmitted diseases, it is helpful to talk about how other common diseases are spread. Review how people get common diseases (Most are spread from person to person.) For example, the common cold is spread from germs that are passed by sneezing into the air, which is then breathed in by another person, or by sneezing onto the hands and then touching another person. A person can get poison ivy by touching the leaves of a poison ivy plant to the skin.

   UNDERSTANDING SEXUALLY TRANSMITTED DISEASES

2. ■★ Sexually transmitted diseases (STDs) are diseases that are spread by germs through having sexual contact with someone who has the disease. (In the past, they were called venereal diseases.) The only way to catch an STD is through sexual contact with someone who already has the disease.

Be explicit about describing the sexual contact: vagina and penis, vagina and mouth, penis and mouth, penis and penis. Anatomically correct dolls are useful for this.

3. ■★ Review the names of STDs, identifying both the slang words and medical terminology, for diseases such as human papilloma virus (HPV), gonorrhea, herpes, chlamydia, syphilis, and AIDS.

   TYPES OF STD'S

4. ■★ Other important points about STDs:

□ = Basic   ■ = Advanced   ☆ = Younger   ★ = Older

> If you have not had sexual contact (as described above), you do not need to worry about having caught an STD.

> If you are thinking about having sexual contact with a partner, consider how to prevent the spread of STDs, such as:

> Asking your partner if he or she has a disease of the sexual parts.

> Using safer sex practices, such as using a condom or having no contact.

> If you find out that your sex partner has an STD and you have had sexual contact, you should be checked by a doctor, even if you don't have symptoms.

5. ■★ Review the symptoms that may indicate that something is wrong and should be checked by a doctor or nurse practitioner, including discharge from the penis or vagina that is different than usual and sores, rashes, itching, blisters, or pain around the genitals. Sometimes these symptoms are due to an STD and sometimes they result from causes other than an STD, such as a urinary tract infection.

SYMPTOMS OF STD'S

6. ■★ You might want to specifically discuss human immunodeficiency viral (HIV) infection. Include in the discussion:

HIV/AIDS

> The serious nature of HIV infection, the course of disease, and treatment.

> Routes of transmission and risk behaviors. People can get infected from blood-to-blood (including blood transfusions and sharing needles when using injectable illicit drugs) or sexual (e.g., multiple partners and not using safe sex practices) contact.

> Emphasize the importance of being able to talk to your sexual partner. This means that you must know them well enough to know their sexual habits and whether you can trust them to be honest about being infected and to use safe sex practices (i.e., condoms or abstinence).

> Present correct information and dispel misconceptions, such as the misbelief that HIV can be "caught" by shaking hands with a person who is infected. For more specific information on teaching about HIV infection, you may want to invite a guest speaker from the local Public Health Department or other agency who is

 = Basic  = Advanced  = Younger = Older

knowledgeable about STDs. It is important that the speaker be able to present the information at a level that participants will understand and find useful.

Goal 11: Discussing Other Health Issues Related to Sexual Awareness

Activities:

1. ☐ ■ ☆ ★ Review the importance of keeping the entire body clean and that body changes at puberty (e.g., acne, the need for deodorant, and menstruation) may mean that you have to bathe, shower, or wash more often.

   HYGIENE

2. ☐ ■ ☆ ★ You may also want to discuss the importance of eating healthy foods, getting enough sleep, and exercising for health.

   HEALTH BEHAVIORS

3. ■ ★ Discuss the effect of using drugs (including prescription drugs) and alcohol on judgment about sexual behavior. Youth who are under the influence of alcohol or drugs (including prescription drugs) are more likely to lack judgment about engaging in sexual intercourse and find themselves in dangerous situations, such as being exposed to STDs or being a victim of sexual assault.

   DRUGS AND ALCOHOL

4. ■ ★ Discuss the pressure from peers to use drugs and alcohol and how it may affect judgment about sexual behavior.

☐ = Basic   ■ = Advanced   ☆ = Younger   ★ = Older

Section 6:
Assertiveness

Goals and Activities

ssertiveness is highly valued in our society. Learning to communicate and behave in ways that protect our personal interests and preserve our dignity is something we all seek and value. When youth develop skills to express their needs, desires, choices, and opinions, they can then protect themselves from exploitative or abusive relationships and develop and sustain healthy relationships. For example, the behaviors involved in meeting new people—extending, accepting, or turning down a social invitation—all require assertiveness.

Being assertive is especially difficult for youth who have been taught to be dependent, passive, and compliant and to trust others' opinions about what is best for them. It is best to foster choice making, encouraging the opportunity to practice and make real choices in both small and important areas of the youth's life.

While assertiveness training should include "stranger danger" concepts, the focus should be on learning to be assertive with people with whom youth have ongoing relationships or contact. Because we know that 90% of sexual abuse of people with developmental disabilities occurs at the hands of someone the victim knows, it is crucial to help youth assert themselves with friends, family, and support providers. In circumstances in which the youth is highly vulnerable (e.g., those with profound mental retardation), the family and support providers need to be responsible for careful screening of caregivers and assuring a safe environment. With the extensive use of social media, the risk for exploitation or abuse should be acknowledged.

Research tells us that victims of sexual abuse are frequently chosen not because of their sexual attractiveness but because of their perceived powerlessness and nonassertive demeanor. It should not be surprising that people with developmental disabilities are frequently viewed as easy targets. Sex offenders assume that people with disabilities will not understand what is happening to them, will not be able to defend themselves against assault, and will be unable to tell others about the incident. To counter these assumptions, personal empowerment must be an essential part of any program aimed at preventing abuse.

Goal 1: Increasing Self–Empowerment Through Words and Actions

Activities:

1. ☐ ■ ☆ ★ Talk with youth about how we express our feelings and let others know what we want or need. Have children practice using their words and demonstrating actions that they can use to tell others what they need, want, or don't want in socially appropriate ways.

   EXPRESSING FEELINGS, WANTS, AND NEEDS

2. ☐ ■ ☆ ★ We can also let others know our opinions and feelings through words and actions. Gather several pictures of food, clothing, or games. Model how to express an opinion by holding up a picture and saying a statement, such as "Mmm, I love pizza," while holding up a picture of a scrumptious pizza. Have children pick a picture and voice their opinion, either positive or negative.

3. ☐ ☆ ★ Role-play situations in which children express their needs or desires. For example, your mother prepares a turkey sandwich for you every day, but you really love peanut butter and jelly. Practice asking your mother to make a different kind of sandwich.

Goal 2: Recognizing a Situation as Potentially Dangerous

Activities:

1. ☐ ☆ ★ Help students identify dangers in their everyday life. Danger is something that is not safe and that could possibly hurt you. For example:

   DANGERS

   ➤ Playing with matches.

   ➤ Playing on a street with lots of traffic.

   ➤ Going in deep water if you don't know how to swim.

2. ☐ ☆ ★ Talk about feeling safe and unsafe. Discuss times when you knew you were safe. What did that feel like? Talk about times when you felt unsafe, frightened, or embarrassed. What caused those feelings?

   SAFE AND UNSAFE

3. ☐ ■ ☆ ★ Review "strangers" from Goal 2, Activities 15–17, in the section entitled "Relationships." A stranger is anyone you do not know and whose name you don't know. Some strangers are community helpers and citizens, such as doctors, nurses, policemen, and adults with children. Most strangers are not dangerous. Other strangers may be dangerous or try to hurt you. Dangerous strangers might be hard to pick out just looking at them, so always trust your gut feelings.

STRANGERS

4. ☐ ☆ ★ Review with students the concepts of good, bad, and confusing touches. (See Goal 5, Activity 4 in the section entitled "Sexual Awareness.") Explain that good touches feel nice, like a hug from your mother when you want one; that bad touches feel bad, like a kick in the leg that hurts; and that confusing touches feel strange, like when someone you like who is usually nice to you touches you in a way that doesn't feel right.

TYPES OF TOUCHES

5. ■ ☆ ★ Review trusting your own gut feelings. (See Goal 2, Activities 18 and 19, in the section entitled "Understanding Relationships.") Think about how you feel when you're scared. Your heart pounds, you breathe quickly, and your hands sweat. This means that your body is responding to something that isn't quite right. Sometimes, you may feel these scared feelings when you are around a stranger. You might also feel these scared feelings when you're around someone you know. Listen to those feelings.

TRUSTING A "GUT FEEL-ING"

6. ■ ☆ ★ Discuss sexual abuse. Begin by reviewing sexual body parts (see Goal 3, Activities 4 and 5, in the section entitled "Sexual Awareness") and appropriate and inappropriate touching (see Goal 5, Activities 1-5, in the section entitled "Sexual Awareness"). Use of anatomically correct dolls is helpful here.

SEXUAL ABUSE

> Define sexual abuse, which is also called sexual assault. Sexual abuse is when someone touches the private (sexual) parts of another person or has intercourse with someone without his or her permission or against his or her will. Sexual abuse feels like a bad or confusing touch. It also occurs when someone shows his or her private parts to another person or asks another person to touch his or her private parts for sexual excitement when the other person doesn't want to. The person doing the sexual abuse could be a familiar person or a stranger.

☐ = Basic   ■ = Advanced   ☆ = Younger   ★ = Older

➤ Talk about rape. Carefully explain what it means. Rape usually means vaginal or anal intercourse.

➤ Where can sexual abuse happen? It can happen almost anywhere, so it is important to learn how to identify whether or not you are safe and how to protect yourself from danger.

➤ Sexual abuse can happen to anyone—male or female, old or young.

➤ Who does it? Sexual abuse can happen with a stranger or someone who is familiar to the victim. Usually, we think of dangerous strangers as the people who perpetrate the sexual abuse, and certainly these are people with whom we must be very careful and learn ways of protecting ourselves. However, very often sexual abuse takes place with someone the victim knows. You cannot tell if a person is safe or not based on how he or she looks.

➤ You must trust your gut feelings. There are ways to protect yourself from sexual abuse.

Goal 3: Learning to Say "No" and Using Basic Self–Protection Skills

Activities:

1. ◼ ☆ ★ Review with students the two main ways we express to others what we want, need, and feel: **words**, or what we **say**, and **actions**, or what we **do**.

2. ◼ ☆ ★ Role-play. Help children practice using their **words** to say "no." Sometimes you say no gently, and sometimes you say it very strongly.

   ➤ Start with situations in which youth can practice using a gentle no, such as being invited to do something that you don't want to do.

   For example: Your friend asks you to go bike riding. You are tired and don't want to go. Practice saying "No thank you, not today."

   ➤ Include situations in which youth can practice using a strong no, when it seems that someone is trying to hurt you or get you to do something that you don't want to do. Youth must respond with a strong "No."

   For example: A student and a friend are watching TV. The friend starts giving the student a backrub. The friend says, "Why don't you take your clothes off while I rub your back?" Practice saying, "No," and pretending to leave the room to tell someone what happened.

For example: You are on the bus and the young man sitting next to you, who you do not know, puts his hand on your knee. Practice saying "Don't do that," or "Stop that."

Help youth think of other strong statements, like "Leave me alone," "I don't want to," "That is wrong to do," and "Go away."

Include an example from social media. A person you don't know contacts you on a social media site and asks you for personal information. Practice saying, "I don't share that information."

3. ■ ☆ ★ Have students practice saying no in various ways by using **actions**, including facial expressions and body language. To get the idea, you might first show the children a picture of serious, angry, or firm facial expressions, as well as pictures of body postures that express strong actions. Ask children to identify whether the pictures are saying "yes" or "no."

Such **actions** might include:

> FACIAL EXPRESSIONS that say, "No!" like looking serious, firm, or angry and looking the other person directly in the eye.

> BODY LANGUAGE like shaking your head no and standing up straight and tall.

4. ■ ☆ ★ "What Would You Do?" Explain to students that if they use communication (verbal or with an augmentative device) and actions together, the message will be even stronger. Present situations to students and have them decide what they would do or say if that happened. Remember to practice using both communication and actions. You could do this activity by having individuals demonstrate their responses or by having the group respond together. Role-play only the statements that are not sexual in nature.

For example, what would you do if:

> A stranger wants you to go for a walk with him?

> A group of kids tells you to pull down your pants when you are on the playground at school?

> Someone tells you to hit another person?

> The bus driver says, "Come here and sit on my lap"?

> A man shows you his penis and asks you to touch it?

☐ = Basic   ■ = Advanced   ☆ = Younger   ★ = Older

➤ Your babysitter touches you in a way you don't like?

➤ Someone says, "I want to touch your penis (or vagina)"?

5. ■★ Discuss the effect of peer pressure on sexual activity. Adolescents can be reassured that what they do with their own bodies is their business and no one else's. Teenagers need to hear that they have the freedom to make their own choices and that wanting to put off sexual activity is healthy and acceptable. Help youth practice refusal skills for occasions when they may feel pressure to engage in sexual behavior before they are ready. For example, "I like you and want to be friends with you, but I'm just not ready to have sex yet."

6. ■★ Discuss home safety. At home, there are rules that you can follow to help keep you safe. Some youth are capable of learning rules and taking responsibility for themselves, whereas others with disabilities require supervision. Talk about, and then role-play, potentially dangerous situations. Give individualized practice depending on the needs of youth. When doing the role-plays, provide situations that give students an opportunity to practice with persistent strangers. Prompt the various phrases. Remind students to use words and actions. Use of real props, such as a telephone, door, door bell, and computer are best.

HOME SAFETY

Some suggested safety tips include:

Answering the phone

➤ Say "Hello." If you give any name, use only your first name.

➤ Find out who is calling before giving anymore information,

➤ Never say that your mom and dad aren't there or that you are home alone.

➤ If they ask, just say, "They can't come to the phone right now," "They are busy," or "Mom is in the shower."

➤ Ask if you can take a message or tell them to call back later.

➤ Never continue to talk with the stranger. Hang up if they keep asking more questions. If the phone call is obscene (the person uses dirty language or says nasty things), hang up.

□ = Basic   = Advanced   ☆ = Younger   ★ = Older

Answering the door

➤ Never open the door unless you know the person (a family member or friend). Do you recognize the voice? Can you see them through a peep hole or window? If you are not positive, DO NOT open the door.

➤ Never say that you are home alone. Just say, "My mom can't come to the door right now."

➤ If the person asks, never give your name, age, or phone number. Just say, "I don't give out that information."

➤ Never leave your door unlocked if you are home alone. Lock the door (with a chain, if you have it), as well as the ground-floor windows.

Social media

➤ Never give out personal information, such as your address or phone number. Just say, "I don't give out that information."

➤ Never send pictures of yourself or your friends to someone you don't know.

Goal 4: Knowing How and Where to Get Help at Home and in the Community

Activities

1. ☐ ■ ☆ ★ List safe people or "helpers" who could provide help when needed. Emphasize that police are often not immediately available when help is needed, so other safe people should be identified, such as bus drivers, store clerks, neighbors, and teachers. If your community has the "Helping Hand" program (in which family houses are identified by a sticker that designates a Helping Hand in the window), describe and demonstrate the symbol.

COMMUNITY HELPERS

2. ☐ ■ ☆ ★ Review Goal 2, Activity 17, in the section entitled "Understanding Relationships." Refer to **Community Helpers**, page 12 of **Me and My World Scrapbook**.

3. ☐ ■ ☆ ★ Dealing with emergencies. What is an emergency? Include fires, accidents, health problems, and robberies in your discussion.

☐ = Basic   ■ = Advanced   ☆ = Younger   ★ = Older

What to do in an emergency? Discuss with parents what each child's plan is according to his or her capabilities. Consider whether the child is capable of staying home alone and what he or she is capable of if the adult he or she is with is injured or needs help.

Role-play to practice getting help by using a telephone to call 911 and asking an adult for help. For example, would you call 911 if ...?

4. ■★ Discuss possible ways of getting help in an uncomfortable or dangerous situation. Such situations might include someone who is trying to hurt you, when there is a fire, and if you are with an adult who has had an accident or injury.

Ways of getting help may include:

> Making a noise or yelling to attract attention.

> Walking or running to where there are other people.

> Using a telephone to call for help.

Goal 5: Reporting Sexual Exploitation or Abuse

Activities

1. ■★ Complete **Safe People**, page 15 of **Me and My World Scrapbook**. Have children identify five people to go to for help. When listing people, think about whether you think they would listen to you. Do you think you could go to these people and tell then what happened?

   SAFE PEOPLE

   Help children think about what they would do if the first person they tell doesn't believe them or won't help them. Make cards with phone numbers for people such as counselors, social workers, relatives, teachers, bosses, and adult friends that they can carry with them.

2. ■★ Role-play reporting potentially abusive behavior or sexual abuse.

   REPORT-ING SEXUAL ABUSE

   For example, someone asks you to touch one of his or her private parts. Practice talking to someone about it. Talk about what youth would do if the first person they told did not believe them.

 = Basic    = Advanced    ☆ = Younger   ★ = Older

Section 7:

Appendix

1. **Sample Letters to Parent or Guardian**

   a. **Describing Sexuality Education Program**

   b. **About Relationships**

2. **Glossary**

3. **Resources**

4. **Expressions (Faces)**

5. **Male and Female Drawings**

6. **Me and My World Scrapbook**

1a. Sample Letter to Parent or Guardian Describing Sexuality Education Program

(DATE)

Dear Parent(s):

Your child will grow and change in many ways within the next few years. Most children are naturally curious about this process of "growing up," and it is perfectly natural for them to be interested in learning about it. We have developed a unit of study to help children better understand this process.

It will include the following information:

1. Understanding human growth and development.

2. Understanding the anatomy and physiology of the male and female reproductive systems.

3. Discussing the physical and emotional changes that take place in boys and girls during puberty.

4. Discussing menstruation and personal hygiene.

5. Discussing communicable diseases.

The school nurse and your child's teacher will be teaching this unit together.

A parent information program has been developed to provide you with an opportunity to view the materials that will be used in this program. School staff members will be available to answer any questions that you may have on the content of the unit and how it will be presented. The program will take place **date**, at **time** pm in **Room #**.

A parent may exempt their child from part or the entire unit by submitting a written request to the child's teacher or principal.

If you have any questions or concerns, feel free to call XXX-XXXX.

Sincerely,

(Teacher or Principal)

1b. Sample Letter to Parent or Guardian about Relationships

Dear _____:

We will be learning about how to appropriately respond to different people in our environment. We will be discussing different types of relationships and appropriate interactions. For example, when greeting others, with whom and where is it ok to kiss, to hug, to shake hands? We are asking for your help in providing us with specific names of people with whom your child interacts and places your child goes so we can use accurate information. Students will be making a scrapbook called **Me and My World**, so any photos would also be helpful.

Student name: _____

Immediate family members: _____

(Please give first name and relationship)

Current household members:_____

(include any non-relatives)

Significant extended family:_____

(Grandparents, cousins, etc.)

Close friends: _____

(include family friends)

Friends: _____

(include adult friends, like Brownie troop leader, etc.)

Some acquaintances: _____

(e.g., neighbors, church members, dentist)

Places frequented:_____

(e.g., daycare center, church, parks, beaches, stores, restaurants)

If you have any questions, please be sure to call.**XXX-XXXX**.

Thank you for your help.

Sincerely,

2. Glossary

AIDS: Acquired immune deficiency syndrome, a serious sexually transmitted disease that scientists believe is caused by the human immunodeficiency virus (HIV), which attacks the immune system (the body's built-in defense against disease), allowing serious infectious or cancerous conditions to develop. It often leads to death.

Abortion: An operation done by a licensed doctor to end a pregnancy before the fetus is ready to be born.

Asexual: An adjective or noun describing someone who experiences little to no sexual attraction. The level of sexual attraction experienced varies for each asexual person.

Assigned gender: The designation given at birth on the basis of a baby's sex organs that determines its gender. In Western cultures, this assignment is either female or male.

Birth Control: Is used when a heterosexual couple wants to have intercourse but not get pregnant. Also called, "contraception" or "family planning." There are several types of birth control, including condoms and "the pill."

Bisexual: An adjective describing someone who is sexually and/or romantically attracted to two or more genders.

Bladder: The place inside the body that holds urine.

Cervix: The opening of the uterus or womb that goes from the vagina and into the uterus.

Clitoris: A small sex part above the opening of a woman's vagina that feels very good when rubbed or touched. It is about the size of a small pea.

Climax: The height of sexual pleasure. In a man, semen usually squirts out of his penis, which feels very good. For the woman, it feels very good to her clitoris, her vagina, and throughout her body. It is also called orgasm or "coming."

Condom: A birth control method for men. A man puts a condom on his hard penis to catch the semen when he ejaculates. Another word for condom is "rubber." A condom is also used for safe sex to prevent the spread of sexually transmitted diseases.

Contraception: Birth control methods.

Discharge: An unusual white or yellow liquid that drips from a man's penis or comes out of a woman's vagina. It may mean that there is an infection.

Douching: Squirting water or other liquid made for douching into the vagina to clean it. It is not birth control and does not keep a woman from having a baby.

Ejaculation: When semen squirts from a man's penis during an orgasm ("coming").

Egg: A tiny cell that comes out of one of a woman's ovaries each month. It will grow into a baby if a man's sperm joins with it. It is also called an ovum.

Erection: This happens to a man's penis when he gets sexually excited. The man's penis gets bigger, harder, and sticks out from his body.

Fertilization: When a man's sperm combines with an egg, which is inside the woman. The fertilized egg will grow into a baby inside the woman's uterus.

Gay: An adjective describing a man who is sexually and/or romantically attracted to other men. It can be used to describe the entire community of gay men ("the gay community").

Gender-affirmation surgery: A broad category that refers to a variety of gender-affirming procedures undergone by some transgendered individuals, such as hormone and breast augmentation therapy. Individuals may seek any number of these procedures, while others may have no interest in undergoing surgery or hormone therapy. Being transgendered is not dependent upon the desire to undergo gender-affirmation surgery.

Gender expression: How one expresses his or her gender via clothing, haircut, mannerisms, and other traits.

Gender identity: One's inner sense of gender(s) or lack thereof.

Genitals: The name for the sex organs or sex parts that are on the outside of a man or woman.

Heterosexuality: A sexual orientation in which a person has or wants to have sexual relations with a person of the opposite sex. That is, when a man has or wants to have sex with a woman or a woman has or wants to have sex with a man.

Homosexuality: A sexual orientation in which a person has or wants to have sexual relations with a person of the same sex. That is, when a man has or wants to have sex with a man or a woman has or wants to have sex with a woman. Another name for homosexual is gay (for men) or lesbian (for women).

LGBTQ: Acronym for lesbian, gay, bisexual, transgender, and queer. It represents the queer community, with the Q enveloping lesser-known identities.

Lesbian: A noun for a woman who is sexually and/or romantically attracted to other women.

Masturbation: Rubbing or petting one's own sex organs for pleasure. Both men and women can masturbate. It does not hurt, it feels good, and it must only be done in private.

Menstruation: Having a period. Blood and fluid come out of a woman's uterus and through her vagina for a few days every month. She wears a tampon or pad during her menstrual period. It begins during puberty.

Orgasm: The peak of sexual excitement for both men and women. Other words for orgasm include climax and come.

Ovaries: Two very small sacks inside a woman's body that hold her eggs. Each month, one egg leaves one ovary, goes through the Fallopian tubes, and into the uterus.

Pansexual: An adjective or noun describing someone for whom gender is irrelevant in matters of sexual and/or romantic attraction.

Pelvic examination: An examination of a woman's sex organs by a doctor or nurse, who looks inside the woman's vagina to make sure that she's healthy.

Penis: A man's sex organ that hangs between his legs. Semen comes out of the penis when it is hard, and urine comes out of the penis when it is soft. The penis is put in a woman's vagina during intercourse.

"The pill": A kind of birth control for women. If a woman takes a birth control pill each day, exactly as a doctor or nurse tells her to, she most likely will not get pregnant.

Prostate gland: The part inside a man that makes most of the semen.

Queer: An adjective used to encompass the entire LGBTQ community. It may also be used as a specific sexual orientation or gender identify or expression.

Questioning: An adjective describing someone who is unsure about his or her gender identify, gender expression, or sexual orientation.

Rape: When a person is forced by another person to have sexual intercourse when he or she does not want to. Anyone who is raped should call the police and get help from a rape center right away. Rape is a crime. It is one type of sexual assault.

Scrotum: The wrinkled sack of skin that hangs below a man's penis. It holds the two testicles, which make sperm.

Semen: A thick white liquid that comes out of a man's penis when he has a climax or orgasm. Sperm is in the semen.

Sex organs: Another name for genitals or sex parts.

Sexual assault: Also called sexual abuse, which is any kind of forced or tricked sexual contact. Sexual assault includes sexual contact with children by adults, incest, rape, same-sex assault, marital rape, and acquaintance rape.

Sexual intercourse: The act of a man putting his penis into a woman's vagina. Babies are conceived through sexual intercourse. It is usually done by two people who care about each other very much.

Sexually transmitted diseases (STDs): A group of diseases that people can get through sexual contact. STDs range from mild to severe and include gonorrhea, syphilis, genital warts, genital herpes, and AIDS. Currently, availability of successful treatment for these diseases varies.

Sperm: Tiny cells that are made in a man's testicles. If one sperm meets with an egg, which resides in a woman's body, a baby will start to grow.

Sterilization: An operation that a doctor performs to stop pregnancy from happening. It is also called "tying tubes," or tubal ligation, for women and vasectomy for men. After sterilization, a man will no longer release sperm to get a woman pregnant or a woman will not be able to have babies.

Testicles: The two small "balls" inside a man's scrotum. Sperm is made in the testicles.

Transgendered: An adjective describing an individual and community of individuals whose gender identity and assigned gender are incongruent. For instance, an individual's assigned gender may be male, but her gender identify may be female.

Urethra: The tube that carries urine out of the body in both men and women.

Uterus: The place where a baby grows inside of a woman. The blood of a woman's period comes from the uterus. Another name for uterus is "womb."

Vagina: The opening between a woman's legs that leads to the uterus.

Wet dream: When a boy or man ejaculates while he sleeps. It sometimes happens when he is having a dream that sexually excites him.

3. Resources

There are many resources available, including curriculum, books, videos, and other audiovisual aids to help educate youth about positive sexuality and preventing abuse. Here is a sampling of resources that may be helpful to you.

Program/Curriculum

CIRCLES: Intimacy, Relationships, Social Boundaries & Social Skills Training Curriculum
By Marklin P. Champagne and Leslie Walker-Hirsch

This is a very useful curriculum to help teach students with special education needs the essential social and life skills directly related to intimacy, relationships, social boundaries, and personal safety. A simple multi-layer circle diagram is used to demonstrate the different relationship levels that students encounter in their daily life. There are three different CIRCLES programs: Level 1 Intimacy and Relationships, Level 2 Intimacy and Relationships, and Stop Abuse. The programs are in video format with accompanying teaching materials. Published by Stanfield Co.

To order the above materials from James Stanfield Co. or to request a catalogue, contact:

James Stanfield Co.
Drawer: WEB
P.O. Box 41058
Santa Monica, CA 93140

Telephone (Toll-free): 1-800-421-6534
FAX: (805) 897-1187
Website: http://www.stanfield.com

Books

Adolescents on the Autism Spectrum: A Parent's Guide to the Cognitive, Social, Physical and Transition Needs of Teenagers with Autism Spectrum Disorders
(2006) by Chantal Sicile-Kira

This practical guide offers strategies for parents to help their children, whatever their ability level, move through the physical and emotional changes of the teenage years. Published by The Berkeley Publishing Group.

Asperger's ... What Does it Mean to Me?
(2000) by Catherine Faherty

This is a workbook that can be used to explain self-awareness and life lessons to youth with high-functioning autism or Asperger's syndrome. Available from Future Horizons (www.FHautism.com).

Asperger's Syndrome and Sexuality: From Adolescence through Adulthood

(2005) by Isabelle Henault

In this comprehensive and unique guide, the author shares practical information and advice on issues such as puberty, sexual development, gender identity disorders, couple's therapy, guidelines for sexuality education programs, and maintaining social boundaries. This book is useful for parents, teachers, counselors, and individuals with Asperger's syndrome. Available from Jessica Kingsley Publishers (www.jkp.com).

The Boy's Guide to Growing Up: Choices & Changes during Puberty

(2012) by Terri Couwenhoven

Written at a third grade level for boys who are 9–16 years old and have intellectual disabilities, this book includes facts and information to help them navigate puberty. Published by Woodbine House.

A Girl's Guide to Growing Up: Choices and Changes in the Tween Years.

(2011) by Terri Couwenhoven.

This book is for girls with intellectual disabilities and helps them learn about changes in their bodies and feelings as they grow up. Published by Woodbine House.

How to Talk with Your Child About Sex: Help Your Children Develop A Positive Healthy Attitude Toward Sex and Relationships

(2007) by John Chirban

This book is a helpful resource for parents regarding how and when to discuss sexuality with children. It helps parents clarify their own thoughts about the topic of sexuality and learn how to guide their children in developing the confidence, integrity, and honesty necessary for understanding sexuality. Published by Thomas Nelson, Inc.

Navigating the Social World: A Curriculum for Individuals with Asperger's Syndrome, High-Functioning Autism, and Related Disorders

(2001) by Jeanette McAfee

In this book, the author provides a definitive program for developing social cognition, with forms, exercises, and guides for students and significant educational guidance and supportive assistance for caregivers and teachers. Available from Future Horizons, Inc.(www.FHautism.com).

The New Social Story ™ Book, REVISED & EXPANDED 15th Anniversary Edition and Comic Strip Conversations

(2015, 2000) by Carol Gray

The New Social Story ™ Book, REVISED & EXPANED 15th Anniversary Edition is a programming resource that involves the development of simple stories in which the child is a main character and the other characters represent actual people in a real-life situation. Using visuals and carefully chosen words, it promotes social understanding and teaches communication skills for a wide variety of situations. The stories are good tools for teaching positive social interaction.

A Comic Strip Conversation is a conversation between two or more people that incorporates the use of simple drawings, which illustrate on-going communication and provide additional support to individuals who struggle with comprehending the quick exchange of information that can occur in a conversation. A basic set of symbols is used to illustrate social skills that are abstract and difficult for students with autism to understand.

Both books are available from Future Horizons, Inc. (www.FHautism.com).

Taking Care of Myself: A Hygiene, Puberty, and Personal Curriculum for Young People with Autism

(2003) by Mary Wrobel

Useful for teenagers with autism spectrum disorders, information is presented in a clear, simple format similar to that in Carol Gray's The New Social Story ™ Book, REVISED & EXPANED 15th Anniversary. Teaching topics include hygiene, health, modesty, physical development, menstruation, touching, personal safety, and masturbation. Available from Future Horizons, Inc. (www.FHautism.com).

Unwritten Rules for Social Relationships: Decoding Social Mysteries through the Unique Perspectives of Autism

(2006) By Temple Grandin and Sean Barron

This enlightening and thought-provoking book is useful to educate those on the autism spectrum and their caregivers about surviving and thriving in the social world. Having been diagnosed with autism themselves, Temple and Sean lead the reader through their mistakes and the ways they found to improve their lives. Available from Future Horizons, Inc. (www.FHautism.com).

Organizations and Resource Centers

Alliance of Genetic Support Groups

4301 Connecticut Avenue, NW, Suite 404   1-800-336-GENE (1-800-336-4363)

Washington DC 20008-2304   Fax: 202-966-8553

E-mail: info@geneticalliance.org   Web Site: www.geneticalliance.org

This organization serves as a referral agency that connects people with genetic disorders and their families with appropriate support groups. It does not offer any direct counseling. Referral services are free of change.

The Arc of the United States

500 East Border Street, Suite 300   817-261-6003

Arlington, TX 76010   Fax: 817-277-3491

E-mail: thearc@metronet.com   Web Site: TheArc.org/welcome.html

The Arc is a national organization focused on people with intellectual disabilities, with state and local chapters throughout the United States. The website has helpful information about diagnoses, services, and advocacy.

Girlshealth.gov (Office of Women's Health, U.S. Department of Health and Human Services)

Girlshealth.gov was created by the Office on Women's Health (OWH) to help girls who are 10–16 years old learn about health, growing up, and other issues they may face. Girlshealth.gov promotes healthy and positive behaviors in girls, giving them reliable and useful health information in a fun, easy-to-understand way. It also provides information for parents and educators to help them teach girls about healthy living.

National Prevention Information Network (NPIN) Centers for Disease Control (CDC)

http://www.cdcnpin.org

This is a United States reference, referral, and distribution service for information on HIV/AIDS, STDs, and tuberculosis. The network produces, collects, catalogs, processes, stocks, and disseminates materials and information on the above topics to organizations and people working in those disease fields in international, national, state, and local settings.

PACER Center

4826 Chicago Avenue South   612-827-2966 (Voice/TT)

Minneapolis, MN 55417-1098   Fax: 612-827-3065

                                                 Web Site: www.pacer.org

This Minnesota-based parent-to-parent organization has published numerous items of interest for families of children with disabilities.

Planned Parenthood Federation of America

www.plannedparenthood.org

This website is the official gateway to the online Planned Parenthood community and a wealth of reproductive health and rights information, including numerous services and resources. Planned Parenthood believes in the fundamental right of individuals throughout the world to manage their own fertility, regardless of income, marital status, race, ethnicity, sexual orientation, age, national origin, or residence. The goal of Planned Parenthood is to ensure that sexuality is understood as an essential, lifelong aspect of being human and that it is celebrated with respect, openness, and maturity.

Resource Library: Center for Parent Information and Resources

http://www.parentcenterhub.org

This website serves as a central resource for information and products of the Community of Parent Training Information centers, with a focus on children with disabilities and their families. It now includes the library of materials related to sexuality and children with disabilities, which was gathered by the National Information Center for Children and Youth with Disabilities (NICHCY). This information was transferred because the NICHCY was discontinued due to a loss of funding.

The Sexuality Information and Education Council of the United States (SIECUS)

www.siecus.org

SIECUS affirms that sexuality is a fundamental part of being human that is worthy of dignity and respect. It provides information and training opportunities for educators, health professionals, parents, and communities across the country to ensure that people of all ages, cultures, and backgrounds receive high-quality, comprehensive education about sexuality.

Community Resources

The following local community or state agencies may be helpful in developing a sexuality training program for children and youth with autism and related neurodevelopmental disorders.

Rape Crisis Centers

State Departments of Education

Family Planning Agencies

State Boards on Developmental Disabilities

Public Health Departments

AIDS support networks

Resources for Internet Safety

Youth are using computers and other devises in school, at home and in places in between school and home. Advances in computer and telecommunication technology allow our children to reach out to new sources of knowledge and cultural experiences, but may make them vulnerable to exploitation and harm by some individuals

The same technology that helps our children to learn can be used to lure or corrupt them. Below is a list of government and organization websites that provide Internet safety information.

A Parent's Guide to Internet Safety from the FBI

http://www.fbi.gov/publications/pguide/pguidee.htm

Internet Safety

http://Kidshealth.org/parent/positive/family/net_safely.html

Safety Tips for Surfing the Internet

http://www.brightfutures.org/mentalhealth/pdf/families/mc/safe_internet.pdf

Internet and Computer Safety

http://www.nnedv.org/internetsafety.html

Teaching Students about Online Safety: Resources for Teachers and Families

http://powerupwhatworks.org/technology/teaching-students-disabilities-about-online-safety

4. Expressions (Faces)

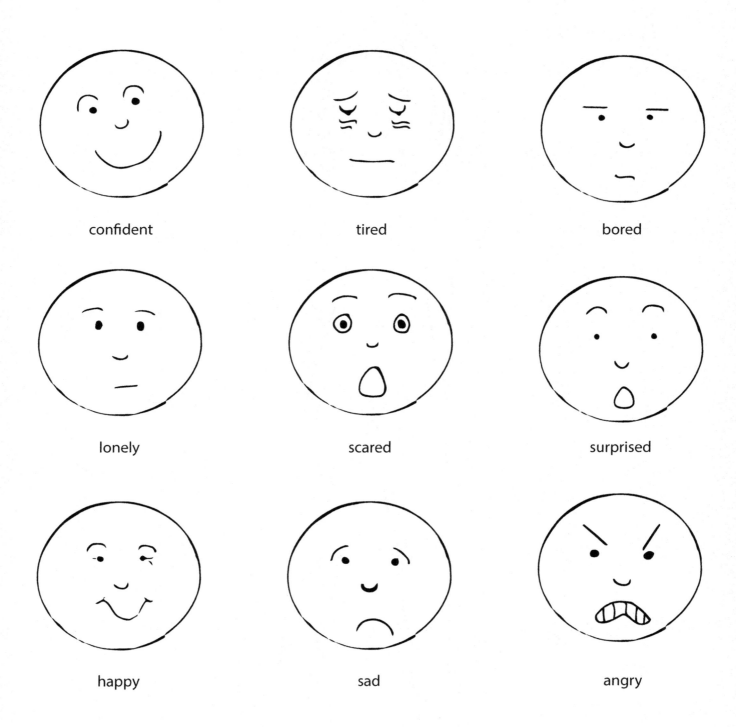

confident

tired

bored

lonely

scared

surprised

happy

sad

angry

5.   Male and Female Drawings

Female Child

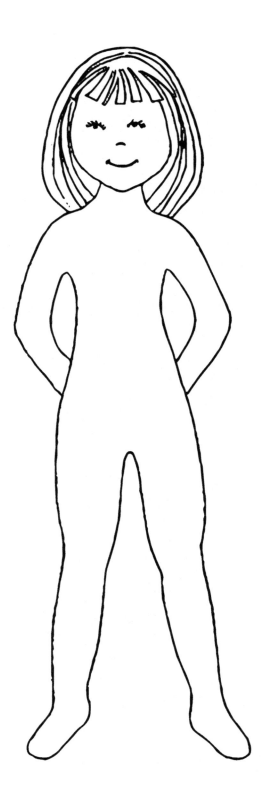

Male Child

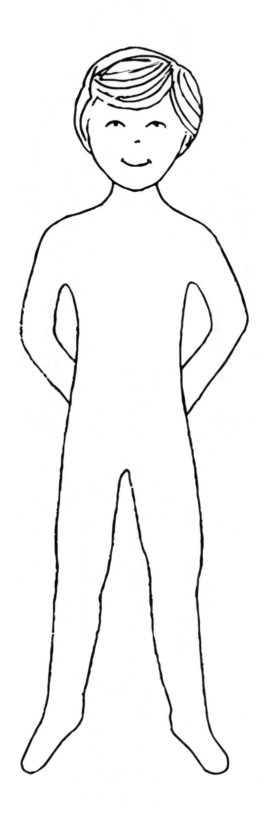

Female Adult

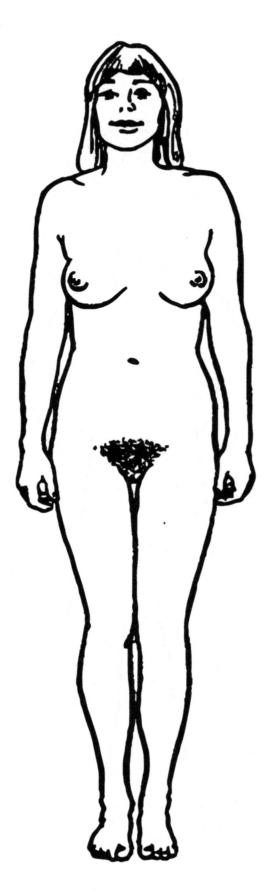

Male Adult

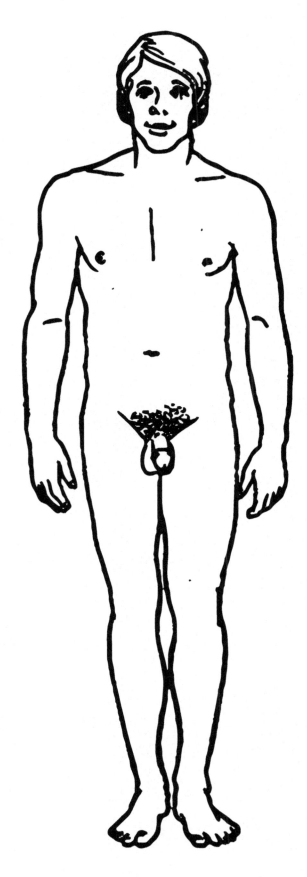

Me and My World
Scrapbook

This is me.

(photo or drawing of yourself)

I have _____ **hair.**
              color

I have _____ **eyes.**
              color

I like to _____.
                                    activity

I can _____.
                            skill or talent

I am like others because I _____

_____

_____ .

I am unique because I _____

_____

_____ .

My favorite things.

Use pictures, drawings, or words to tell about your favorite things—activities, people, toys, food, places, etc.

I AM PROUD.

I am proud of myself when I _____

_____

_____

_____ .

When I'm grown up.

Use pictures, drawings, or words to tell about what you would like your life to be like when you are an adult.

My Family

**Use pictures, drawings, or names to tell about who
is in your family.**

My Family Tree

Paste cut-out apples with names of family members on the tree.

Cut out apples for Family Tree.

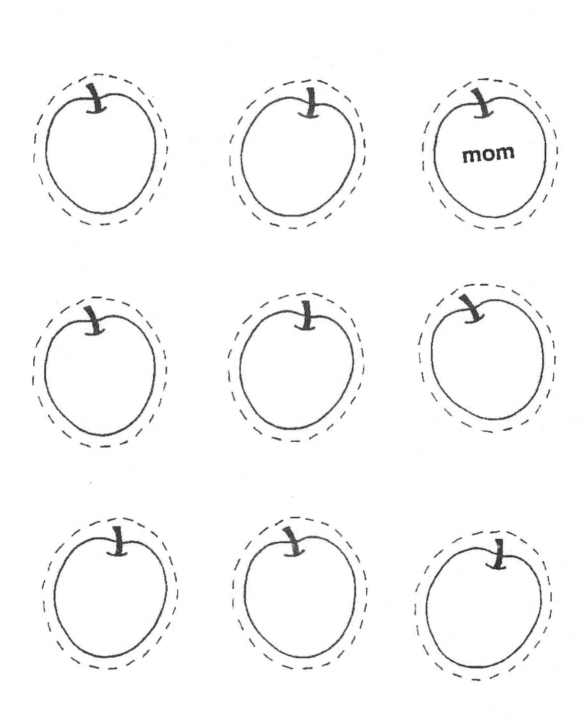

Who lives at my house?

Use pictures, drawings, or names to tell about who lives at your house.

My Friends

Use pictures, drawings, or names to tell about who your friends are.

Acquaintances

**Name people you are acquainted with
in these settings.**

at school

in my neighborhood

in my community
(church, shopping places, recreational)

Community Helpers

**Use pictures, drawings, or words to tell about
helpers in your community.**

CPSIA information can be obtained at www.ICGtesting.com
Printed in the USA
BVOW09s1553250316

441584BV00002B/2/P

9 780986 067327